SONGS
of
LOVE
and
HORROR

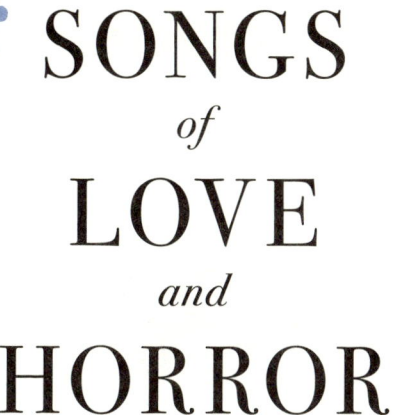

SONGS
of
LOVE
and
HORROR

COLLECTED LYRICS OF
WILL OLDHAM

W. W. NORTON & COMPANY

Independent Publishers Since 1923

NEW YORK   LONDON

For information about permission to reproduce selections
from this book, write to Permissions, W. W. Norton & Company, Inc.,
500 Fifth Avenue, New York, NY 10110

For information about special discounts for bulk purchases,
please contact W. W. Norton Special Sales at
specialsales@wwnorton.com or 800-233-4830

Manufacturing by LSC Communications, Harrisonburg
Production manager: Beth Steidle

ISBN: 978-0-393-65120-1

W. W. Norton & Company, Inc., 500 Fifth Avenue, New York, N.Y. 10110
www.wwnorton.com

W. W. Norton & Company Ltd., 15 Carlisle Street, London W1D 3BS

1 2 3 4 5 6 7 8 9 0

for those who carve out space in life for music

"The music is made to express what we cannot say otherwise."
—CHARLES DUVELLE,

in conversation with Hisham Mayet

CONTENTS

XV

INTRODUCTION

I wanted to be a better singer. I wanted to be a greatest singer. These song words here collected are some of what I thought would aid me in this venture.

Some were meant to be sung low with a big open throat and others to be sung quick and thin, with equal resonance. Resonance is the goal of every song-maker, resonance to an audience, and first to the singers.

If something is too specific, its light burns out quickly. If the words are exceedingly oblique then the light never catches. The lines of a song get put together with the knowledge and hope that those lines will be sung very many times before they're forgotten and disappear. The words themselves and how they fit together ought to intrigue and seduce the singer, and present little challenges that can be pleasurable for the singer to greet. And then what you feel when you sing . . . well, there are pathetically few songs that can come through without a sympathetic instrument* to deliver them. Lyrics are disguises or costumes for emotions, memories, problems, exclamations . . . so that all of these intangibles can walk among us and be welcomed as civilized and recognizable. Right? In order for anger to be presentable, you have to cloak it in words. Lyrics demonstrate that we, as singers, are at least trying to get along.

It isn't song-writing so much as it is song-building. Making up songs. I started into this line of work when it was plausible to make a life out of it. We made songs on one side of a line and on the other side was the audience, the listeners. Anyone

---

* "instrument" here means a voice and the means to use that voice

can make up a song. The challenge was in navigating the gate-keepers and getting a song in a suitable position for folks to hear it. My understanding of what I wanted to make had to do with the very individual experience of listening to performed and constructed recordings.

When I got to know records and recorded music, the process went like this: we sought out music, we found music, we brought this music into our world and there we spent lots of time with it. It grew on us and became a part of us. It sat visibly and tangibly in our spaces and demanded some small amount of care to maintain. So then when I started to be a maker of these things, I approached the endeavor with concern and with lots of attention. The records and recordings I loved were sloppy, raucous, demented, devastating, random, precise. What allowed the makers of such works to be able to bring such life to me?

Here in this book are the lyrics for many songs. The lyrics could be called the bones of song at times, the flesh of song at others. I like to think of a song as something you can carry in your brain and then re-present its essentials to someone else using just the voice. This is because I am really only a singer with really only my voice; what guitaring I do is done with the awareness that the guitar signifies absent others.

The primary intention of these works is to provide platforms (or excuses) to commune with others: with people I love, musicians I revere, and audiences who feel similarly desperate for connection.

SONGS
of
LOVE
and
HORROR

AFRAID AIN'T ME

Scorn me not though I deserve,
I've done fighting in my time.
"Long live the people!" hear me shout,
And tell my enemies I'm blind now.

Trust to me your little ones,
Slow and sweet I teach.
Woman-man in blended garments
Try to block my greatest moments.

Cold and clear,
Alone I may be,
But afraid ain't me.

All the little black ones
Know and shout my name
All the little white ones
Think this is a game

Treat me well when wandered to your door
Bathe me please for I am dirty
Wash me hard with scalding tears
And with bath water drain my fears.

The lack of urgency with which
folks approach life is
astounding

1

AFTER I MADE LOVE TO YOU

eloquent, I soon retire
to nothing else I may aspire
after I made love to you

in the dark I see you glisten
to your breath I lay and listen
after I made love to you

in your arms I'm softly resting
memories of you undressing
and your lips my final blessing
I never knew the embrace that I'd been lacking
has been found with kisses smacking
and two bodies there attacking:
I and you

baby, why don't we feel guilty?
why's it seem we're doing right
when we're doing something filthy
in a rented room tonight?
I think it's 'cause we love the now,
we love forever love, and how!
and my life's your love anyway
and your life's my love every day.

you are mine o now forever
think of you always wherever
after I made love to you
after I made love to you

Written to live among the duets of
Conway Twitty and Loretta Lynn

AGNES, QUEEN OF SORROW

If you wait another day
I will wait a day

If you wait another day
Okay. Okay.

Every time I think you say
It's time for us to go our way
I say wait another day

Got a letter that did say
That the kid had passed away
And everything it didn't say

If you wait another day
I will wait a day
If you wait another day
I will wait a day

Time has got me in its sway
And though I'd like to ride away
I will wait another day

Some things need to be said again and again.
Many things. Most things.

AIN'T YOU WEALTHY, AIN'T YOU WISE

Ain't you wealthy, ain't you wise?
Ain't you made to give to me?
Ain't it all good,
Good enough to sing . . .?

It's a wondrous day to see
The joy I hold in me while I leave

Now you've seen the evil eye,
Hold on to me while I cry

The moon is very low,
It watches while I go
Where I go

Bound in blankets and blond hair,
You'll be shocked to find me there

Ain't you wealthy, ain't you wise?
Ain't you made to give to me?
Ain't it all good enough to sing . . .?

There's no pain to lament
And no dream undreamt
There's no pain to lament
And no dream undreamt

> Do you answer these questions if you hear them sung?

ALL GONE, ALL GONE

if you think I should go
I really will go
if you think I should go
I really will go

now the preparation's made
to lay all old things by
and when I say that I'll go
I mean let one name drop away

all gone

O I see you can shake that thing . . .
let's have some of it over here
it's tragic that your love is long-crossed
but we can fix it up with some beer.
it's a dream to really be here with you
it's one in the morning, just going on two
with nothing but just to snuggle and coo
it's a great thing, a really cool thing to do

all gone

if you could stay on the wild kicking horse
I could handle your presence beside me
the dust is a must, so is doubting my trust
so is acting haphazardly

hey hey

> An early "real" song that could live to play among
> other real songs until it grows into a proper old thing
> and decays & dies or makes a fool of itself.

5

ALL IS GRACE

The blessed grace of waking up
Of breathing in the sheets
And hello to you, at the window
Hello to you

Down the hill I'd like to take you
To where I shot a little deer,
My little dear
I'd like to take you down there

Rinsing out the iron cup
To have a glass of wine
To have an iron cup of wine, dear,
to drink it down there

A drunken pair
Goodbye, despair
One night is 'til one morning
And once at night
you held me by
and held me until it was morning

And once the temperature did fall
Goodnight to Father, Mother
My bambina was all and for a while

All is grace tonight to you
And tomorrow we will be,
And tomorrow we shall see,
And tomorrow, too

Intended to sound like the doodle-doo
of a Norwegian folk song, sung to
obliterate the drudgery of everyday tasks.

ALWAYS BATHING IN THE EVENING

Screaming
Jump in
Waving
Jump in

Wade in
Wade in
Get in

Blowing
Jump in
Waiting
Jump in

Wade in
Wade, wade in
Fouling

Bathing
Swimming
Fouling

Singing
Drinking
Clapping
Moving

Sleep in
Lay in
Jump in

There's sex, there's singing,
and there's swimming.

ALWAYS BOUND

My road is elusive
I can't leave my skin
I would leave what's intrusive
But that's all that's ever been

Always bound

It sucks to have erased
Any idea of home
So all of my decisions
I have to pretend they're my own

Always bound

Bound to be traveling
Bound to be true
Bound to unraveling
What binds me to you

Stay with me, stay away
Leave things as they are
Leave your hurt in my throat
Leave your soul in my heart

Always bound

To build a ballad like this,
look at parent/child dynamic
and run with it,
& keep running.

ANOTHER DAY FULL OF DREAD

I like to have a good time;
Any of my friends will tell you.
So if you confront me with stupidity,
I'm doubly angry at you.

So I become more lively
To bury all of the ugly.
Whole persons sometimes
Must be, them bodies, buried.

And I sing "NIP NAP!
It's all a trap! BO BISS!
And so was this! WHOA WHOA!
To Haiti go, and watch it all come down!
DING DONG!
A silly song sure do say something's wrong
Smile a while, forget the bile,
And watch it all come down."

and I toe the water
and an urchin poke me
and I must be godfather
to anyone who'll have me.

Today was another day full of dread,
But I never said I was afraid.
Dread and fear should not be confused;
By dread I'm inspired, by fear I'm amused.

Bonny was born smiling & laughing, making jokes of the darkest
& worst of things. This is one song I remember singing in Jacmel.
The other singer on the balcony ended every song with a quiet
declaration, in heavily accented English: "Thank you, Jesus."

9

ANTAGONISM

I went someplace where some friends and I
Spent some days in the years that had gone by
And one was there, it seemed by chance
On the left side of the beach blowing on his hands
While I sat on a right-side rock
Glancing over, caught off guard and slightly shocked:
How could I have known that he would be there
Fixing the water with an aimless look?
He didn't see me, that much was sure
But that didn't help me feel any more right.
We'd been close, it had been a long time ago,
and I had hardened myself, and him . . . I do not know,
He just stayed soft and never seemed to grow.

Just for a moment
Does it ever dawn upon thee
To do things for me?

Swinging back from one chord to another,
Try to focus, I'd learned from my mother,
Who'd also taught me to take care of others,
When I could, if I could, like if they were my brothers.
But I never found it much in me to care
If god give someone their absolute share
Of the good that they deserve if they choose not to
Recognize value in the things that they do.
I've seen people crumble and fall by the way
And humble themselves like it's their due to pay,
But I ask myself: why not act harshly?
Why keep awful thoughts and feelings inside of me?
Why not mete them out ever so generously?

Just for a moment
Has it ever dawned upon you
To do things like I do
And sabotage your rightful due?

L. Ron Hubbard said that his
money/power grab scientology was not
meant to help the insane because
"the insane . . . well, they're *insane.*"

APOCALYPSE, NO!

We dined in the breezeway
And met later in the carport for drinks.
We rationed out the pills,
Splitting evenly the blues and the pinks.
We didn't really split the blues,
I only mean that's what he thinks.
He got the mother lode this time.
Why, o why are best friends such finks?

We met on the causeway
Unloading all our grievances there.
He pat me on the shoulder
And I playfully ruffled his hair
Then brought him to the waterline
And constrained him while he struggled for air.
Then I pulled him back and kissed
And we both went arm in arm to the fair.

> The beginning came from D. C. Berman,
> the rest rushed out in an effort to
> describe some parts of our complicated
> dynamic.

ARISE THEREFORE

There will be no end soon, if I've seen things right that
    have come.
People will be scared they never will see anything,
Meanwhile all of my friends have been struck dumb.
How can no final thing come when our faces are pulled
    from us?
How can someone blame who they refuse to name
For pulling other people down with them?
Some have risen. They are lucky to have their fall delayed
    by people.
What they have is threaded, grafted, and plotted,
Played out and bad.
Some have made mistakes for us, waiting by the door for us.
We told them to go ahead; their support is just a weight.
Better to sever the weighted limb.
Where is it hanging tonight?
It is not looming to propel us along.
We move ourselves to it, one year to sit in dirt,
One cycle with which to comment upon the dirt.

> The title comes from an old Indian
> book, referring to something about the folly of
> defining morality. This song is one
> of my favorites. I'm told the melody
> was stolen from Sinéad O'Connor and
> I can't deny it though it was not
> intentional. She has been very sweet
> to me in dreams.

AT BREAK OF DAY

i know the sun's about to come up.
i close my eyes anyway.
my mouth is dry and the sheets are cold
and will be still come break of day.
you called me up just to surprise me,
to hear my voice, see what i'd say.
i only whispered then hung up.
i whispered, "wait till break of day."

i locked my door, i should unlock it . . .
what if you should come this way?
and in and have a drink and dancing,
dancing till the break of day,
and then to bed we'd dance towards
and tiredly kiss and roll in hay,
but waking in the evening i see
you left after break of day.

at the break of day i'm ending all of it
and so don't say you've had a ball.
dawn is mine but i will share it
with whatever bird will wear it
on her body bare and pink.
now what do you think of break of day?

i hate myself when i'm alone.
it's just with you i feel ok.
so tomorrow you'll feel sorrow
when i am gone at break of day.

I'm not cool with
the disengagement implied
at the end of this song.

AT THE CORNER OF THE STAIR

At the corner of the stair
Will you always be there?
Will I find you even if I don't want to?
Neath the old willow tree
With my pants at my knees
Will I find you singing so gently?

Saying you love me
And you want me
And you'll always be mine
But you'll hurt me
And you'll use me
To get out of your bind
Will you shuck me
And discard me
When I've served my time?

And will I be waiting for you?

There's a room that I know
And I know how to go
If I want to hold you helplessly
At the corner of the stair
In the dark waiting there
For the day when we're able to see

That it's ugly
That it's not me
Holding court in your eyes
That your body
Has destroyed me
With its harrowing cries
That you got me

If you want me
But god knows it's unwise

To go down this hard road again

Here we go
It's not love anymore
Don't you say that it's love
It's not love anymore

At the corner of the stair
Were you going up there?
Were you thinking that I would be waiting for you?

I was walking outside
In the clear mountain air
There's a little girl waiting for me . . .

Big ballad born of a title given
by Oscar Lee Riley Parsons.

BE STILL AND KNOW GOD (DON'T BE SHY)

One night while walking on the rounds
One seems to lose all control
The face jerks in a spasm of frowns
And the blood on the shirt
Ladies' faces and memories of things
Tried to long put away
Surprised the head and a number of things
Seemed to subtly say:

O don't be shy

I can glance with a movement of lids
Or a shift of the head
When confronted with things that I did
Act like nothing's been said
Or take god as a covering guard
When I do not believe
In the grace of a governing god
Who can see us in need

I love my god

Help me find what it is to be
Is a womanly cry
Any hint of a request for help
Is not from I
I can sing on the corners of streets
O so in love
While some goat incessantly bleats
From there above:

O don't be shy

a formula:
cat stevens + mekons + old testament
equals
danceable desperation

BEARGRASS SONG

Water and fire
Strange bedfellows when they roll as one

Water and blood
Trading death for life as they roll away

Water and life
Where does one end and the other begin

We named it Beargrass
It rolled before us
It rolls among us
It will roll after we're gone

Beargrass Creek flows a few blocks
from where we live. I first sang
about it in a translation of
Broeder Dieleman's "Gloria."

BEAST FOR THEE

Why aren't you kind to me?
You could so easily
Take me in your arms and see
A donkey . . .
a beast for thee.

If you had half a mind
Leave worldly things behind
Devote to being kind
You to me:
a beast for thee

Love in some way you choose
God's plan can easy bruise
One bone-and-blood mass we fuse
And I can be
a beast for thee

I will toil for years and years
Give you muscle tone and tears
Overcome and flay all fears
Leaving me
a beast for thee

And at home on Wednesday morn
Astride my horny horn
You'll be in glory born
And I will be a beast for thee
Happily a beast for thee
Quietly a beast for thee
Endlessly a beast for thee

The donkey is Balthazar, who
replaced the Green Arrow in my
hero-scape. Because who wouldn't
give herself to a long-eyelashed
bouquet-bearing scruffy ass.

BED IS FOR SLEEPING

Bed is for sleeping
Love is for making
And you know, love, I am yours for the taking

My eyes are for seeing
The wind is for blowing
And you see, love, I am yours for the knowing

Night is for dreaming
Sleep is for bedding
I will dream with you the night of our wedding
You have a splinter, and I have a thimble
I will pull it in with movements so nimble

Tears are for falling
Smiles are for breaking
Houses for burning
And kisses for faking

And where are you going?
And why are you leaving?
Left on the walkway
To swallow my grieving

Try to keep things out of the bed
that don't belong there. Things
like insecurity, anger,
+ big heavy books.

BEEZLE

Now I will say what I needed to say
Destruction of hate begins today
I won't box
Nor stand down, get slugged,
Nor have shallow breath
Nor lay and be drugged
I'll stand up to evil
Body and soul
Not die at thirty-two
But live to be old
I love your voice
Also your eyes
Finally finally hopefully wise

Bring me a daisy
Show me the Mississippi
Disappear with me
I live because you love me

I used to be desperate to know what
was going to happen in life to me.
To know *something*. This song
marks a beginning of embracing
uncertainty.

THE BEST OF FOLKS

Don't argue with a fool for she will hurt you
The best that you can do is step away
Don't tie yourself to children, they'll desert you
Fools & children live as if it's just today

Much contention causes losses and estrangement
Isolation is a sickness unto death
Loss of love is a sure pathway to derangement
Which is why I say make peace with every breath

If you're asked to do a favor by your brother
Even if it is an overwhelming task
Don't ignore it, nor exchange it for another
Undertake to do it just because he asks

Mention misdeeds of a loved one in his presence
Lest a deadly peril claim his every hair
When a cherished one is mentioned in her absence
Say what she should want to hear if she were there

You'll meet friends through other friends and they'll be stronger
The way to trust and faith is faith and trust
Revere those first friends for their love is longer
Fool the devil, for the devil's way's a bust

Don't get angry if you're called the worst of many
Don't withdraw your hands from all that they can do
Those who would deny your love may not have any
For the best of folks will see the best in you

Lessons from a book on brotherhood
read too late by too few.

BEWARE YOUR ONLY FRIEND

I want to be your only friend.
Is that scary?
My active mind don't wish it so,
But you should watch out for the silent thoughts;
That's where the seeds of soul-sucking grow.

You want to be my daughter.
(Come sit up on me)
I hate it but I also know it's so.
And I wanted you to be something like a mother,
Cheering me as I go.

When each who comes around you takes some of your light,
That's when I get angry,
An 'outfit' for my fright.

Picture us lounging,
Sitting and listening,
And loving what we hear.
That will never happen.
We both flail too much
To let the other near.

I want to be your only friend.
Beware of me.
My quiet mind is not fit to lead.
Take the warning that I've seen fit to lend,
And from this thing that we have be free.

Some crave mutual reliance,
some are repulsed by it.
It doesn't matter. The bridge
here implies that, in this situation,
both stances are impossible.

25

BIG FRIDAY

You saved me from melting, baby
You saved me from stinging and being holed up
And braking in snow and killing more
And overspilling my runneth cup

You had light in your hand and your eyes closed
You had movement out of my sight
You wore no shoes and ate like a leopard
And slept with your legs apart every night

And if I had to live
This is what it should be:
To have such a woman with me

When tidal wave hit and our house was in splinters
I thought you had took all you had to take
But you snuggled to me on the ground in the winter
And your breath smelled like honey in the frosty air wake

A song can help transform wild optimism into blessed reality.

BIRCH BALLAD

I set out one morning to go and find your life
For it was my intention to one day be your wife
It was my intention to have you as my own
And so I made a road to you and went that way alone.

I knew, to be completely yours, that everything should go
I undressed and stood there in the cold and falling snow
I undressed and made my parents too ashamed of me
To ever love what I once was or what I am to be

You see me through your window, you see me in the dark
You gently pull the curtain to, and vivisect your heart.
The hatred that you feel for you is equaled only by
The love that's curled here rising in the hollow of my eye.

Will we meet and will we speak and will I be your life?
The wind it makes my flower weep, the rain it cuts my mind.
I'm eating you, I'm feeling you; your old life, it is gone,
Because I made a road to you and came that way alone
Because I made a road to you and came that way alone.

Written for Björk to sing, then
rudely reclaimed to build
a song with Matt Sweeney.
In my defense,
our jam was a B-side,
B for "barely a blip."

BLACK

Black, you are my enemy
And I cannot get close to thee
Our life is ruled by enmity
And I can't weaken that
The only way that I can see
Is to hold you close to me
To love you for it's meant to be
I weaken your attack

Everything was luked and downy
What was good was up from under
Until Black, that awful tender
Came and popped my sense of wonder
All at once all eyes turned at him
Leaving me an unwatched body
And it sagged, my body's rib cage
Out from under ogler's study
Black was decomposing quickly
This was found offensive to me
His disrespect for life's proprieties
Made me scared he would destroy me

So I thought I'd try to cut him
Try to force him neath my level
The only way to equal to him
Would be hit him with a shovel
But to really rise above him
That would be the final evil
So instead I asked the sucker
If he'd care to see my rooms

And as a friend and as a comrade
And all the things that these implied
I made him leave what it was that he had
Used to keep us unallied

Now Black and I we are together
Fairly just inseparable
And in the terriblest of weather
Our bonds are incorruptible

In dreams I fight with you.

BLACK CAPTAIN

Ever see someone do so well
That none could ever stop him?
Commanding o'er the hardest swell
With no force or fault to top him?
Well, under all and every one
Is hidden a woman or man
Who lights and inspires such higher desires
And allows him to do what he can

I was his true and he made my fortune
He led from on top of my shoulder
He could lead pure when my worship was sure
And many times even step bolder
He loved me and needed, saw trouble and greeted
For trouble is best met head-on
What seemed so distinguished became plainly vanquished
When I left to find life on my own

Now men laugh at him and say
That better men number in thousands
Nobody ever goes out of his way
To lessen his clouds as they crowd in
And I am nearby and I watch with a sigh
As my captain curls up like a cripple
And hope that he goes where nobody knows
Under sea and leaves not a ripple

What power he has only I know
And now I have let my captain go

Nothing great is done by one.

BLACK CAPTAIN
revised for Peter Willcox

Starting from last couplet, verse two:
When he'd disappeared into hazard I'd feared
I was now meant to sail on my own

There is a place on the open sea
You will say it is like any other
It has an air of importance to me
As it waits for the hull of my brother
It had been my thought that the power he got
Couldn't be there without what I gave him
And now I find a good part of my mind
Will be worthless unless I help save him

He ain't here ain't here
I can't handle this lack
And now
I want my captain back

written for Peter Willcox,
captain of the *Arctic Sunrise*,
during his 2013 Russian detention

BLACK DISSIMULATION

sweet ill health has hidden from me
events about which one has no memory.
whether it is to pretect or dony
one is not told and one asks not why.

the noise near the trees gathers into a block.
one drinks just to where one is able to talk.
tries to confuse things that surely occurred,
by stretching and acting like one hasn't heard.

blank indiscretion and testing of lines
at the end of a farm there to kick it.
to find a dead dog, swollen and bald
and to giggle and poke it and stick it.

to sit in the drive and pull a head down,
or to push in the way of an oncoming blow.
to take wine on holidays when no-one's in town
to dislike someone and let them so know.
well, I let it burn out this morning at home
the stove and the kitchen; the howl and the steam.
and lay on the couch, sometimes resting alone
in order to utter a decorative scream

disgust and disgust, and a pretense of light,
persistent denial, way late in the night.
ignoring the stupid and hating the silent
disliking the prurient, disdaining the violent.

denying the rice and accepting the drink.
however it comes at the start of a fall.
take it whenever you get it, you think;
you're unlucky ever to get it all.

you're rude to the relatives; cold to the friends
unpleasant to god when he comes by the house
one tries to across as the storm it begins
and goes to the inlet to see things out

High school.

BLACK ICE CREAM

such noises from all over
let them have their fun
you and I know in our hearts we are the only one
asleep in my arms your hair smells fine
what we did when we were free was have a good time

I met you when I was free, in summer it was
you were there with your father, as everyone does
and I bought you an ice cream, cold and black
you curtseyed a 'thank you' and I bowed back

good times should not be took for granted
my lips upon your hands were pressed
waves roll and rolling over laughing
sandstorm and star-storm at once

what we did when were free was have a good time

at night by the water you asked me for a kiss
one fond one for parting and we promised we would miss
and then came the sunrise and noises burst forth
you had become mine and there was nothing more

what we did when we were free was have . . .

> Should have called it "Summer Loving"
> or "Atlantic City Girl." Anything
> but "Black Ice Cream."

BLINDLESSNESS

I can't see what I am doing
It's like a dog is standing on my face
Like I have been stabbed in my lower spine
My legs in the dregs of a sorry place

And if the dog would weigh a little more
Stand a little harder
I would give in

Luck is a storm that flails
In the tropics where I have never been
Thunder is the sound
That others hear when they win

And if it would
Rain a little harder
Blow a little more
My heart could cave in

I've heard others suffer under
A weight they love to wear
Why can't I take what I have seen
And get far away from here

If I could
See a little farther
Live a little more
I'm sure I would win

Begun at the instigation of
an Austrian filmmaker, who
abandoned it, mewling at
the hospital. We nursed it
and now we love it.

35

BLOOD EMBRACE

Oh god, would I give her up to him
If she told me he was better
And that I didn't have the chance
That he did to impress her?

Does she test me? Does she know?
That I would sooner turn and go
Than fight another, if that is what she'd have me do

And would she stop and hold me near
If she could see the future here
Would hold me if she held me to her too?

I would not fight with hands or words
Another man, no, that's absurd
Or would I? and would victory betray me?

Or is that what she's waiting on?
A pounding down, one standing man
To kiss her in a blood embrace of victory
To kiss her in a blood embrace of victory
To kiss her in a blood embrace of victory

Oh god, would I give her up at all
Because I know it could not be better
To live without what she provides
When we're alone and I undress her

Does she test me? Does she know
That I would never turn and go,
But fight another, if that's what she'd have me do?

Or is that what she's waiting on?
A pounding down, one standing man
To kiss her in a blood embrace of victory
To kiss her in a blood embrace of victory
To kiss her in a blood embrace of victory

Trying desperately to navigate
another's trauma. When in
doubt doubt doubt: sing sing sing.
When sad or afraid: same. Do the same.

37

BLUEBERRY JAM

When life is tough and very scary
My wife and I, we chomp a blueberry
When hardship comes, well we don't tarry
We rush to the fields and pick some blueberry
When future days are hot and hairy
When Christmas threatens to not be merry
When weighted down with more'n we can carry
We drop everything and eat a blueberry
When the liquor cabinet's out of sherry
And no-one can answer my eternal query
And I can't reach my dear aunt Teri
I know I can savor a juicy blueberry
When world leaders act like Moe, Curly, and Larry
And even the Buddhists get leery and wary
And there's too much falling to dodge and parry
Why not relax and try a blueberry
When the hatchet you threw in the hole won't stay buried
        And the last bus left for Tucumcari
And the world feels like a mortuary
        Everything's just too temporary
Everyone's creamer's gone non-dairy
        The Devil's joined the seminary
When the rivers flood at Harpers Ferry
        And the voices are silent in Tipperary
Wife asks "ready?" and you scream "very!"
        Let's be smooth like Fred Astaire, he
Wouldn't waste no time
I'll eat your blueberries
You eat mine
We'll be fine!

    We rose from bed to the news that a ballistic missile attack
was underway. It wasn't. Instead the indomitable generosity
of friendship flooded in, everybody wielding blueberries.

38

BOLDEN BOKE BOY

If I move slowly through this task,
I will earn some rest.
If I move quickly and surely,
I will do my best.

I'm sad to see things change for you who were such
    good friends.
One should walk the way one needs,
And when the way is crooked, one bends.
Out that evening (it makes me sick to think),
You put your hands up, as if to say:
"I won't be part of what you do.
Life ain't war, least not today."

This is how it would be, when we would meet often to see
How easy things could be made
And still go down unanxiously.
Once you were chased down the street by blacks
screaming about how cool it is to be black,
and you ducked away.
It will never be as cool as this.

Then it was needed to become rough
In order not to be inhuman,
Uncanny, unable, and unwilling
To think about not having children.

For Brian McMahan.

BONNY'S ARK

I want to save all the animals
Before it starts to rain
I wanna march them two by two into this song
I want the kids to know their names

LIONS SERPENTS
EAGLES COWS
SKUNKS AND RATS AND SPIDERS
THE WOLVERINE AND MOUSE
GIANT SQUID AND HONEY BEAR
MOLES IN THE GROUND
KILLER WHALE
POCKET WOLF
RHINOCEROS AND HOUND

When the rains come, we'll be there
To sing them in the sky
Make constellations with our song
Together, you & I
They'll remind us of eternity
So they won't have to die
They fill our dreams with savage schemes
We'll join them by & by

HUMPBACK WHALES
CROCODILES
GOLDFISH AND GIRAFFE
STARFISH ANTELOPE AND DEER
THAT WILD HYENA LAUGH
HUMAN BEING, COCKATOO
ELEPHANT AND BEE

YOUR MOMS, YOUR DADS,
YOUR PENGUIN BIRD
YOUR FIRST BEST FRIEND AND ME

I'm starting to think that
the whole ark story might
be better for us
after all.

THE BRUTE CHOIR

A cow called, then they all called together
Describing the way to go
I never hurt someone so young
And I never held someone so sweet.
It makes me want to holler with them all the way down.

All the way down
Their voices show the way
How to hold it back and see the end of the day
Shut the mouths, shut the mouths
And rip the pictures down.
Withdraw, withdraw,
You live so far from town

This is what makes a thing last:
How to make what didn't happen go.
Take fear
And call it lust
And let me go lay in the snow.
I cannot rest with so many singing
So many songs and what a way to sing.
Their voices are bringing the trees to their knees
With nothing to say when they're speaking.

The choir, the choir, their voices go higher.

There are so many more singing now. Juxtapose, in your
mindbrain, a phonograph recording of
Mabel Mercer or Enrico Caruso with your own,
or your grandmother's, or your neighbor's
singing & then realize the balls-out nuttiness
of how singing is experienced today.

CAL'S SONG

Don't want no-one to call my own
No black elephant I would have to push away
One to not be there one evening when I get home
Making another evening threatening and gray

What has made this feeling in my mind?
What even allowed my body to be here?
Right punishment is what I find
And that's just what bonny old me does fear

For everything that I've come to fear and loathe
I've done many times to one already
And I quake at night to every telltale noise
Of what I know must be justice creeping stealthily

Lord you take your stranglehold
And squeeze the living out of breath
Beat the smiles from my mouth
And break the springing from my step
The very tone my own name rings
Inside my head
Will be silenced when you
Put the life in me to bed

O lord I will be good in heaven
Call me to sit at your right side
It's only earthly sin
Because it's earth I'm in
I stand by my doing and don't hide

The bad brother's song.

CARELESS LOVE

I wrote a careless love,
"Love me not, for I'm above,
above a cloud all flat and white
and with another love tonight."

And then a careless love
By weighty cloud above
Was ground into the floor
To loving breathe no more.

Lady when I leave you
Limp on the floor
Distorting our voices
Slamming the door
I say "sorry"
I say "bye bye"
I say "miss you"
I say "cry cry"

The opening stanza is a ticket-buy,
the song looking for a place
among nursery rhymes & waulking songs.
It's just awful enough to imagine a
long life in eleven-year-olds' heads.

44

CAT'S BLUES

I'm gonna turn my back for a while, now
while nothing bad can or will befall
the lights welcome me all by myself
and the fires only bronze they do not burn

well do you understand girls where it's going
o girls, that there's violence to come
happy now, o so happy now
but crying ere the night has come

children in the fields, they play, they reel
scolded when they come home, dirty, crying
Well, love is forbidden outwardly
but inside there is no denying

so do all the shy boys bury their heads
and they shuffle while they waste and hurt
they are men who bow before us now
and I do not trust them, no

How many children are there like this?
Yes, and how many will I serve?
o if I could have a clue what justice is
it would be more than I deserve

time is passing, come into my house
loot the pantries and muss the sheets
ere you've found a useful trinket here
your host will be ten miles on by

Imagining a folk hero named Cat Stevens,
based on the music artist who, at the time,
had removed himself from our active observing.

THE CELLAR SONG

You turned from me, Mother, 'cause you love your man
And I am your daughter, you've given my hand
and you've twisted my arm
And you've shown me the road ahead
Thank god, you've shown me the road ahead

His arms locked in mine,
I find us this morning
My eyes pushed protruding by a hard-boggled head;
The wine you poured to my husband and me!
When may I taste it again, ma?
Tap on the door and leave it outside in the hall.

My eyes stay a-bursting,
The glow and the smell from
My fair skin, now tainted.
The floor planks I know well,
Each creak and each crevice,
The curve of the cask at my back, oh lord!
Spigot-chapped lips small and cracked.

O come jabbing again, old companion
Let's children, together, let's let 'em thrive in the cellar.

A take on arranged marriage:
thank you, sir, may I have another?

COLD AND WET

Water may stop warmth. This do not forget:
When things become too warm, make them a little wet.

Douse them with a mouthful.
Put the baby down.
Clean the earth surrounding and cause the warm to drown.

And introduce to every soul a poultice made of tears,
Hear them bicker, watch them die, impaled on balsa spears.
And looking in the morning
The streets are flooded out
The men are wailing toothless
The ladies ghostly pout
And they shout:

"Our shoes are wet! Our skin is cold!
And we no longer fear the voices of the brave or bold
Making what is to come clear."

Well, future is diminished by what today we did:
We wetted warmth and killed it and in the water hid.

Lie in bed together grateful
that there is a roof overhead
to keep you dry.

COME IN

Come in
For one last dinner
That I will make you.
Come in.
It is a small one,
For I am no cook.

Come in.
You have a long way
Where you are going.
No longer welcome
And I am happy.
Yes I am happy
You will be leaving.
Things will be changing
For you.

You have done much for me
But now you're leaving.
It's back to Egypt
That you are going.
They are not family.
They are not friends.
But a false history
And you aren't sorry.

Come in, come in
Or am I silly
For saying such things?
Am I implying that you
Must come again?

The narrator here addresses Johnny Faa, a gypsy folk hero. The song gives voice to a sister of mercy, along the lines of Johnny Cash's "Come In, Stranger." The "stranger" aspect here is a revelation to the singer who had hoped and assumed that she could sing to this same person forever.

COWS

A house with sign we all know
Welcomed folks to: come and go
Give money, smiles . . . and families grow
The Lord said it shall be so.

But true when sound came crashing down,
And hideous ruled o'er the town,
The house was shut down.

"You're welcome here . . .
but others are not welcome here."

One voice said, "Please come this way,"
Another place not very far.
White walls and no faces painted
Underneath a moon & star.

Fat men smiling, bearded men
With blue eyes shining, doubt within
Human grace has never been, nor will be.

"You're welcome here . . .
but others are not welcome here."

Many wives & many lives,
The smoke don't kill, it reddens eyes.
The time has come to pay blood tithe
To one true god.

Each other are the manifest of moon & star,
"You're welcome here . . .
but others are not welcome here."

Religions are clubs.

50

CURSED SLEEP

I slept sweetly unpretending
that the night was always ending
she breathes lightly right next to me
and I dreamed of her inside of me

and in my dream she sang so sweetly
a melody I hope to sing
so enslaved by her sweet wonder
cut my legs and fingered hunger

she sang my name and so engulfed
and I cried and felt my legs fail
in her arms I trembled electric
and she let me and she held me

then waking she was older still
and holds my love against its will
in spell cast with her palms extended
cursed love is never ended

cursed eyes are never closing
cursed arms are never closing
cursed children never rising
cursed me never despising

oh I am loving always holding
while she sleeps, her song enfolding
epic song it tells of how
she and I are living now

Attic madfolk make for terrible bedfellows.

DEATH FINAL

God bless us as we cross from green sides into darker.
God love us as we lay in puddles of our own.
Our qualities will raise us in a light that blinds our mothers.
Our fists will serve to clear out debris of no mistake.

Summer has me holding little one high in the air.
Oblivious packs of dogs go running over there.
Our beauties tried to crush us, it's strange faces that they wear.
A smile is hidden in the working faces.

In a pit of bodies,
I am loved by all.
By ham hock and by handkerchief
by damsel and by doll.
an Angel warns us with its unfinal call.
It was not death final,
it was only fall.

A hymn, for a shrine built inside
of a television after electricity
has flown away.
Death is the end of earth's music.

DEATH IN THE SEA

Someday I must die
It ain't for me to know why
And I want to die in the sea

So why not go now?
It's simple (and how!)
To put this end to me

Well, I don't really mind
If that's not how I die
So I'll put it off with a gleam in my eye

Blue.

There's a hole in the sky
Through which I must fly
To get to my grave in the sea
To get to my grave in the sea

Another ditty for the children.

DEATH TO EVERYONE

I am here, right here where God puts none asunder.
And you, in black dress & black shoe,
You do invite me under.
Go on, go there;
You can see me aging.
Stars turn,
Balls burn,
Coming kids, they are raging.

Every terrible thing is a relief.
Even months on end buried in grief
Are easy, light times
Which have to end with the coming
of your death friend.

So strap me on and raise me high,

'Cause, buddy, I'm not afraid to die.

Life is long
And it's tremendous
And we're glad that you're here with us.
And since we know an end will come
It makes our living fun.

Death to me
And death to you
Tell me what else can we do die do?
Death to all and death to each
Our own god-bottle is within reach.

Death to everyone is gonna come,

And it makes living
Much more fun.

I am brainwashed to think that life has a beginning and an end,
and that all moments are elements of story with cause, effect. It
is unbearable at times to try to assess
the weight of each plot point and clue.

THE DEVIL IS PEOPLE

I been away, been in some kind of bind
Jump the fence, put order to my mind

Shake the weight of this life off and say,
"There stands the path, it's my first one today."

Do you wonder where your boy has gone?
Obliterate & start over on your own.

What can't go bad?
Something that's already turned.
Ain't no-one sad to see a dead field get burned.

I'm grateful to the fates that I was born.
I found a wet hole in early morning.
I was surrounded by an animal
who sung to me, "The devil is people."

I never knew a song so true.

It swims beyond and I can't swim so low,
And so I let it go.

Beware still waters where the monsters loiter deep.

DISORDER

It's Lisa, or Laura; I know not her real name
Which is probably pretty or something the same
With her I spoke under-, and lived underfed
Without her I hang now, without her instead

We die many times, and each new infancy
Is a surprise; that I have the tendency
To look over when it suits me, and decry when not.
When I am sailing, or when things go well

When this vision of death comes, she always leaves
And I bury my head in my billowy sleeves
To marvel at how I must face my own fate
Or deny it, more likely, until it's too late

When I could have kept on at her, with her, inside of her
Instead of letting her weakness successfully hide her
Her weakness and mine, the death of us both
I was more violent, and she was more loathe

To see in me a promise of what I could give
And I to see in her a reason to live
Which was past just a symbol of woman and luck
That I would never be lacking for something to fuck

And one to fuck over when things would decide
That it was once again time to go for the ride
We felt we must seize the weather, and never the whim
To be led by the other and not the within

My wife is reading the autobiography
of Viveca Lindfors, an actress
who went years before realizing

57

that she had behaved awfully to others,
over & over, in the interest
of her art and ego.

DRINKING WOMAN

A woman who drinks, drinks

And she dances and winks
And she rests her head and thinks
Of drinks

She thinks of drinks and sleep
Though it's hours before she sinks
Into bed and links the things that she thinks
To drinks

She likes to drink
And she loves to lean
And she breathes and bleeds alcohol

Some people, daily, expend
as much energy making themselves up
as they do tearing themselves down.

EASE DOWN THE ROAD

I took her on a simple trip
to see her husband's family
and on the way, upon her hip
was laid my head down gently
all due respect was meant and all
the winds were in agreement
that this was answering the call
of awkward and true feeling

a fireman her husband was
and so to give him duty
I duly tried to light a fire
upon his rightful booty
but beauty was my treasure then
as through the hills I drove her
and taught her that another man
could have made love to her

strange is good if it is kept
a secret with the lovers
who love their mates
and love themselves
and need the love of others

through the window I could see
the fields and clouds all passing
as in the passenger position
Eleanor was thrashing
I stopped the car, we got a beer
and then eased down the road
a little guilt, and some guilt spilt
and added to our load

My mother's siblings
were firemen + firewomen,
firepeople.
We recorded the song in late summer,
Shelbyville, KY
and it's those fields + clouds
that come to mind
when I sing it.

END OF TRAVELING

If you are sleeping, Millie, you are okay.
It won't be me that wakes you up today.
Opening these eyes taught me fresh that I should
Let you crash.
Well, close 'em and I'm gone.

Sleep on. Let me go,
Oh Millie.

One town beyond, I'll lay me down.
You go on and close 'em on this town.
I will be happy to close my eyes on new places,
Or half close 'em with new faces.

And if you are chilly, Millie, it is okay.
You've got enough blankets to warm you in some way.
The chill reminds me soon that some other one will swoon.

I'll go to Mississippi and the last one will be there,
Hitching up her skirt in a wood ladder-back chair.

Oh Millie.

Curlicues & patterned prints,
shirts that fit well an
old man's spine. An old
man who gets his authority
to sing about feelings from the past
from the song itself.

ENDING IT ALL (AS I DO)

Are we square?
I wouldn't like to go
Knowing there is something
Crucial that I owe
No light in my pocket
No trust up my sleeve
A devil is calling
And I take my leave

And take a look at the back of my hand
The last thing you see as it falls away
And try to remember the light on the land
Ending it all (as I do) every day

Home from work
The sounds are immense
Knowing there is something
That will never make sense
No fun in my wardrobe
No moon in my view
Turn and listen to god
As I turn from you

And take a look at the light on the land
The last thing you see as it falls away
Try to remember the taste of my hand
Ending it all as I do every day

One day the task
Will be taken over and won
The beginning of ending
Is already done

It's as if I learned nothing, nothing.

EVEN IF LOVE

Once again in the world,
Of twelve hundred feelings
All in electric lights,
We see what we can

I love the sound of wind,
Blowing at night through trees
From the roof I can see tombs
Past the houses of the city

And I have been yours,
In foul and in praying
And I love to look at you
From the side at night,
With music playing

And love will protect you
To the edge of the wood
then a monster will get you,
And love does no good

And even if love were not what I wanted
Love would make love the thing most desired

Grateful for some of the ways
that Polly Harvey showed
me to sing, the words
and the ways.

FACE HIM

It's a shrouded figure I see
Ahead of me
But when he turns
But when he turns

I've been following for days
Many ways
And when he turns
And when he turns
He smiles
Smiles
He smiles

And the lighter side is shown
And the brighter side is shown

And I face him now
Oh and I face him now
Oh and I face him now
Oh and I

Jesus Judas John Obi-Wan
Marlon Mark E. Smith Mahatma Mrabet
Daniels Pauls Davids & Toms
Dead fathers who return in dreams and dilute loss

FLOOZY

I'll go with anyone
(*Almost* anyone)
Who smiles at me and implies a want inside.
I'll lay by anyone
(Some someone),
Who's kind to me and lets me be the loving kind.

I am that open,
I am that free.
I am as loose as I can be.

When it comes to loving I am a floozy.

I'll take in anyone to anywhere.
You couldn't count the times and names I've laid me down.
But I don't love them
I love someone
And maybe she would love to . . . pal around

I am that open,
I am that free.
I am as loose as I can be.
When it comes to loving,
No-one else can hold me.

But she's so far away
And can't afford to come to me
Will she ever be
More than in my mind?
The one with whom I'm happily
(And admirably)
Her one man?

I worked hard on this song and I love it.
I submitted it as a possible piece for
Merle & Willie to duet on for their
final collaborative album. I doubt they
ever heard it, but wouldn't that be something?

FOR EVERY FIELD THERE'S A MOLE

for every man who will last
there's nothing he can't get past
no obstacle he cannot erase
for every king there's a crown
and every time I look around
I am the king of infinite space

For every field there's a mole
With the soil that he stole
And the sightlessness that lets him go free
For every drought there's a rain
And when my earth's in pain
I watch it boil
O tearfully

There's a time to sing these things
And a time to have them sung
A time to bring the tune
And a time to have it brung
There's a lap for resting head
There's the only nesting bed
There's the souls to cry among
For the things that don't get sung
And a hand to hold your throat
To stifle that crying choke

What a stew: whiskey jingles, Shakespeare,
Bascom Lunsford, lawn pests, climate
change, judgment day.

FOR THE MEKONS ET AL

Is it time for you to settle down?
Yet your tiredness and sadness keep my spirits up.
And the guns and greed that is in your heart
Is what a deputy lives for.

Without you, deputies *exist*;
No voice to broadcast feelings with.
Intuition, luck and fear,
Confusion, age and sweat and beer.

If you won, they'd be the new Mekons
And you, perhaps, a myth bygone.
No, they have something that they can see
And history is there to serve our cause.

Memory, reality,
Loyalty, idolatry,
Money growing on a tree
Picked by aging little men.

Deputies do not rely.
Individual unions,
Imagination, open eyes . . .
They're the new home militia.

Executive branch in a nation of one,
Exercise our power
To veto, veto, veto;
Be the man of the hour.

Laws exist like history books.
Atlantis State University!
If you can forget how to ride a bike
You have had a good teacher.

The words are there like a pretty picture
Hanging on the bathroom wall.
At age sixteen, you are stealing a mirror
And find a friend beside you.

Say your piece incidentally,
And pick a dancing partner,
And follow the steps and don't forget
You can use it again later.

If we drink, we still think
And we wake up in the morning
Or we stay out all night long.

The righteous path is straight as an arrow.

It was said that trying to
describe one's relationship
to Mekons was akin to
describing a dream or
an acid trip.

FOREST TIME

Filling up the girl
I am filling up the girl
Make her all of the whole world
Filling up the girl

And a brand-new baby child
Makes me trunky
Makes me wild
Makes me trumpet of the swan
A brand-new footprint-maker born

I be ashtray, I be star
I be monkey by Babar
I be hippo calling far
Far into the forest

And a shark, I break its back
And an enemy attack
And chompers chomp
And then they crack
And then a baby's eaten

But a baby girl is growing
And all of us over-shadowing
My animal's below-ing
Ocean time
Forest time

Not seeing the forest for the trees,
the ocean for the water,
can be a wonderful horrible state.
It is where we live during
the skillful telling of
a ghost story.

GARDEN OF EVIL

we had enough.
all the world was yours & mine.
of everything that's laid before us
the thing that brought us down was time

these faces, did we create them?
they've been added to by forces.
they'll turn against us,
we don't have to own them,
if we turn strongly towards the west.

I want that devil to be mine,
I want it all the time,
unadorned, naked & free.
but my child don't care 'bout me.
no, my child don't care 'bout me.

we were given life by life
and no-one will take it back.
block on block, they build against us
guarding 'gainst some wild attack.

I wanted that baby to be mine,
completely all the time.
a loving child for all to see
and now my child don't care 'bout me.
no, my child don't care 'bout me

leave the snake to the sky
& the baby to die.
we'll have fun, you & I.
now don't cry, babe, don't you cry.

Written to accompany a comic by Charles Burns + Killoffer.

THE GATOR

It's all from the gator.
It's all from his home.
O I love the gator.
I love him alone.

At night when I'm sleeping I know I'm alone.
And off on the gator I allegedly roam.

Catch heez eyes in the light and leave him alone.

He's off on the gator; that's why he ain't home.

Would all my friends were just like so:
Almost unknown.
I'm off on the gator,
And boy am I stoned

Trumpeting: tu-tu-tu-tu! through a hollowed bone,

Off on the gator, over the homes!

When off on the gator
My dignity's grown.
My eyes are much larger,
The gator has shown.

Reclaiming some of the territory
lost in adolescence. A night
kitchen was built, then abandoned.
Now I am better able
to whip up batch after batch.

73

GET YOUR HANDS DIRTY

get your hands dirty for me

and you will never see
me turn away from what makes you unhappy
and you will never see
me call you a coward

get your hands dirty with me

and I will always be here
trying to be easy
everyone will say
it's good that they treat each other this way

I want someone who'll clear trees for me
I want someone who'll plant peas for me
is that silly? I don't care
I don't keep my shame in there

get your hands dirty with me

all I need's a place to rest
I will take you at your second best
you've made it to my heart

Written for Candi Staton to sing,
and she did.

GEZUNDHEIT

I dreamed I saw Phil Ochs last night
Alive as you or me
Said, "Howdy Phil. You're
fifteen years gone."
He said that he had never died
He said that he had never died

Down to my house, I saw him wandering
I said to him, "You've never
entered my dreams."
He said, "Why should I?"
He asked me, "Why should I?"

"I thought that I had some
sort of bond with you."
"You've none of the kind."
"But Phil, why do I feel this way?"
"You've got an unhealthy mind."
He said that I've got an unhealthy mind.

Self-destructors repel.
Phil Ochs is an exception,
maybe because he tried
to parse so much of it
out in song. Ochs
wrote a song about Joe Hill
to the tune of a song about Tom Joad
which was Guthrie's re-write of a song
about John Hardy.
So this song "about" Phil Ochs
was written to the tune of
a song about Joe Hill.

75

THE GIRL IN ME

HIM:

There's a girl in me that makes me wear bright colors when I
walk the streets.

And there's a girl in me that makes me want to feel you deep
inside of me.

There's girl in me that makes me pose before a mirror like a
movie star,

And makes me want to dance around the pole instead of sitting
at the bar.

HER:

Well, the man in me must love the girl in you.

Because there's a man in me that wants to dominate you and
put you in your place.

And there's a man in me that wishes I had a beard and
mustache on my face.

And there's a man in me that gets short of breath in the girl's
locker room,

And wants you to be the bride and me to be the groom.

HIM:

Well, the girl in me must love the man in you

TOGETHER:

'Cause there's someone in me that sees you without clothes and
sees what I should be.

And heaven only knows what will become of me.

There's someone in me that others knew was not the way that
I should be.

God chose for me a color and lord knows that She may not
agree

That we should explore our mirror sexuality,

But we can share our secrets in our privacy.

The you in me
must love
the me in you.

Just feel comfortable in any bathroom.

GIVE ME CHILDREN

I take in a stranger and he hits me
I take in a wind and it bites
I listen at night to you cry constantly
Saying, "Show yourself. Fight yourself."

We are two kids, we've acted foolishly
When could we possibly?
O when could we possibly?

Only every summer
Then only if you know
O I know, I know
I only know you
And always this will be true

Living on the memory of this love
Memory is knowledge, dove
She leaned back on the wood and she closed her eyes
Saying quietly
As she went to sleep:
"Don't let anyone see us,
say what they've seen and expose us.
I've seen how they are and I hate it.
They could never talk about where we've been."

There was a sense of accomplishment
that came with this song, followed
by a bewilderment with the
fact that life goes on whether
or not there is a sense
of accomplishment.

GO FOLKS, GO

I'm not leaving, I ain't going . . .
you never asked me to!
So I'll sit and smile here with you,
like I never thought I'd do.
Wash the walls and paint the windows,
polish face and shave the shoe.
I got gal and I got friends,
like I never thought I'd do.
I never thought the sun
would rise in the east and set in west;
I figured I owned just dark skies
and that darkness fit me best.
Here I is, all thin and balled-up,
wrapped up in a coat of you.
I ain't hemmed-in, I ain't walled-up;
I am free and I'm loving you.
I can snooze and I can amble.
I can jump when you say 'boo.'
Freedom is a hard-won gamble;
so is holding things like you.
My chest swells and my nose snores;
it's all okay by you.
I've never felt this welcome before . . .
I'd a never thunk, would you?
Serves one right. No need to think.
It will all be laid before us,
and god will guide us to our graves,
smiling, singing (here's the chorus):
Go folks! Go forth! Go folks!
Trust your brain! Trust your body!

Contentedness
bears declaration pretty darn well.

79

GOAT AND RAM

There is no God but God
God in your body which is mine
I'm in love with you, with God
With our children in time

Once you have given your body
And demanded I give mine
We can be, you and me,
With our children in time

Just like anything
Choice is neither yours or mine
To love with all that will be
With our children in time

I can give in to you
Because I know that you are good
I can fall into you
Lay in, love in you, wetting wood

For you, honey love
Sky above
Silver cross
Flower cross

All is. All am. All gives
Goat and ram.

Forever we watch things die
You hold me close, and so do I hold you

Although we walk away
We walk away in time
Rocks along the way, they rock and so do mine

I'm in love
And there's music playing
A whole new love is fully saying

Though fire burns
And wool is woven
The hands may strike but still there's loving

With his music, Matt Sweeney
made this ferocious. It is
inherently an effort to not feel
like such a stranger amid my
own language.

GOATS

It's to ghosts that I turned
And goats that I turned
And goats that I turn
To pass the time
It's not goats that I turn to
Baaaaadly.
I like my friends
I feel unfit for them
It makes me sad
I'll be gone

But where I go
Only my lover knows
Only my ego goes
but we go

It's the loveable lightness
Of seeing the light
Every dog has its say
Every song paid for tonight

Written when the lines between those
realities shared & those uniquely
mine were well-nigh
indistinguishable. And yet
there's something vaudevillian here.

GOD IS LOVE

I'm always scared
Whenever I leave a place
Scared of how
The leaving will change my face
But when I'm gone
I always start to feel
More at home

I'm always scared of seeing you on the street
Frightened of
The way in which we might meet
But when we do
I always seem to feel
Less alone

The one I admire
Lives very far away
I hope that I'll live
Right by her side some day
And when I do
I know that I
Will never mourn

God loves me
God is love
God is everything
And I am love

Made up with the voice of Bill Callahan in mind.
It ends with an optimistic application of logic
to the universal conundrum.

GOD'S SMALL SONG

I will wake up tomorrow
I have tended to God's small song
And to Love's small song
And closed my eyes on a sleep so long

And tonight I'll go
Into all of the places that you love
That is my place here
To have been in those

I will wake up tomorrow
I have amended some of the things
That some actions bring
And closed the head to be with you

In each eye there is an apple
Buried there before the eye
And out of sockets come the branches
And from the branches dangle I

A devotional in the spirit of Baby Dee.
Comfort food for a hungry ghost.

GOOD TO MY GIRLS

We all have ways
To make it seem
We are not hard or bad
I chop down trees
& spit in faces
and laugh when you are sad
your happiness means almost less
than all that's in the world
my existence is okay I guess
because I am good to my girls

I take them to the movies
I put food in their openings
I sew the holes in their lives shut
And temper any hoping
What can I say?
I didn't ask
To own their days and worth
I'm good to them
And thereby earn
My share of life & earth

They may cry
But not to me
They know I wouldn't hear them
Other folks
And family
Hate me and I don't fear them
I fear the fact
That after life
Complete emptiness whirls
We only have our share of life
So I'm good to my girls

A brothel owner sings. She is a lady.

GRAND DARK FEELING OF EMPTINESS

well i felt like i was born today
so i took it upon me to go away
to gather my thoughts and go away
where i could (be used by) somebody
now over the hill, like always you know
were billy and frankie and henry and joe
and they beat and broke me hard and slow
to prove i was nobody
and no-one i was and so remained
knocked-out in a hut, no mother, no name
and filled up my heart with one and the same:
that grand dark feeling of emptiness

and was it a friend that turned me loose?
or was it a girl come to baste my goose?
or was it my great god who laid on his finger
and started my clock anew?
ah no, it was rain
ah no, it was gunning
it was point break and buckle
and singing and cunning
that skinned me, re-skinned me
and started me running
and i never looked back from then on

and now i am learning bit by bit
about the make and model shit
the muddy bowl i live in it
and all the mucks that tire us.
and i'm afeared if i don't have
a piglet, lamb, or little calf
i'll chop my humanness in half

and be as worm or virus
but kids i've had and they are sung
upon folks ears my babes are hung
rhythmically they live among
and grow but don't get old
not in a box, not in a void
not if their voice is never heard
nor if no-one repeats a word
but if their tune is told
then we can age and fall away
to meet again some golden day
and fill it in our happy way
in starlight and in gold

This cartoon is rated X for
adult themes.

A GROUP OF WOMEN

bless his head, his blessed state
has got me crawling neath the gate
to watch them wash, the women there
bless their arms, bless their hair

I shall not be a weight to thee
for I am free, will ever be
future days with future sound
is offering to come around

and as I sit and watch them wash
I have no point to get across
I have no mouth and still I stand
to peck the youngest woman's hand

and glory rise upon her breast
and her breast-breath rise, and so I rest.

The god damn male gaze.

GULF SHORES

It was hard enough to climb upon
It was slow going at first
Sister, you have laid long in the sun . . .
Aren't you dying of thirst?
O my dear your suit is candy-striped
And your legs are long and slim.
If I whisper nothings in your ear
Will you pass them on to him?

You have laid here by the waterside
Since the day we came to town

Have you thought that you could waste away?
You don't care much for yourself
There are circles deep beneath your eyes
Why do you do this to yourself?
If you like, we two could take a ride
I would love to take you down
We could watch a blue heron in flight
We could see the sights in town

You have laid here by the waterside
You have let the family down

A cold and fruity drink awaits us both.
Watch me frolic in the sand.
Oh did you see me in the surf
With a starfish in my hand?
Soon the restaurants will open up,
Soon the bars will light their lights.

You have aged, you must start looking up,
Ugly things will come tonight!

We could drive down to another beach . . .
Even tanned, your skin seems white.
All our friends have gone away from here
So let's disappear from sight

I have never had and can never have
a sister, making such a relationship
a bottomless spring of wild
and woolly exploration.

HAPPY CHILD

I imagine my hands are clean
I am revitalized by things unseen
I begin a dialogue with the road
toothless, hopeful, about to explode . . .

how could I have ever been so lucky
to wake up looking in her face
and see the flowers she put 'round the room
brightening an otherwise crumbling place

she told me that jesus loves me
but I never knew who jesus was . . .
some kid somewhere fucked-up?
well isn't this what a savior does?

don't cry
don't feel
don't die
because death is not real
it's good
it's yours
and it should come when things have run their course

I wanted her melted up inside me
all the tears and the smiles shed for me
she'd disappear to the world around me
everything to be a powerful memory

so I brought her to the swamp she loved so well
where I gently placed her in it
I brought her soul to ease with kisses
and I said to her as I's about to begin it

don't cry
don't feel
you won't die
because I don't think death's real
it's good
it's mine
and it should be
at your heels all of the time

and she said:

"and where's the sky for me now?"   it's good that she sings
"and who will take it down?"   the freedom it brings
"and drape it all around me"   her voice is my very head
"every cloud and cosmo for a gown"

I'm a good kid
old style
a happy child
and I'm never going to have to do that again
but if I want to, I can

don't cry
don't feel
don't die
because death is not real
it's good
it's ours
like the sun
like the worms
like the wind
like the flowers . . .

Take us to someplace murky
and broken, I was asked.
The best-built structures

stay standing, to be
frequented eventually by
questionable entities
who use
bodily fluid
as a
decorator's tool.

HARD IS GOOD

Other folks can say goodbye
That ain't someplace I need to be
My eyes are wide
and so my mind clears the way in front of me
all my paths are paved with grace
all my bills are overdue
I'm saving for a wilder place
Where love commands and evil's through

It's hard—and hard is good
hard—what I always need
hard—and hard is good
And hard comes down on me

Other folks can turn away
That ain't me—oh, hear me sing!
I'll own it all and beg for more
The hardness and the light life brings

It's hard—and hard is good
And almost too sweet
And it's clear to me
That loving you is easy

Age of fire, age of vanity.

Written for Candi Staton to sing. She didn't.

HARD LIFE

I wake up and I'm fine
With my dreaming still on my mind,
But it don't take long, you see,
For the demons to come and visit me.
And I've got my problems.
Sometimes love don't solve them.
And I end each day in a song.

It's a hard life for a man with no wife.
Baby, it's a hard life God makes you live.
But without it, baby, don't doubt it,
You don't even have your tears to give.

I know I'm a hard man to live with sometimes.
Maybe it's not in me to make you a happy wife of mine.
Maybe you'll kill me!
Honey, I don't blame you.
If I was in your place, that's what I would do.

I ain't breathing. Help me breathe. Let me go. Let me leave. I
don't know, but I might lose. I might bum. I might blow a fuse.
Let me go. Lay it down on my own. Let me drown. Let me go
where you don't know.

Got to start somewhere. I
took the baton from Bonnie Tyler
and darted off the field.

HEART'S ARMS

With care from you, I get addicted to
A man helpless and silent.

How can I cry to you?
You'd see my caring ability just tumble.

Why don't you write me anymore?
Have you found something as good just next door?

I open this awful machine to nothing
where once your intimacies came pounding.

Why don't you write me anymore?
What did you bind my heart's arms for?

I hope you find glory in some new heart's arms' story
and can close doors on mine for sure.

The best of the songs
that came from the Headlands,
from a residency there. "Best"
meaning most instructional
and most funnest to play.
The build is like a set of waves.

HEY LITTLE

Hey little one, all you have to do is say
That you need a little help, and I won't be far away
Hey little one, it's more my fault than yours
The life and breath that flows through you,
It was not your choice

But I love you
And I always will

You little thing, you're bigger all the time!
It won't be very long before your shadow crushes mine
And, little one, you may create the day
I never knew could be,
so be gentle on the way
'Cause I love you and I always will

Hey little one, o I get so much joy
Watching over you at night, you're my awesome little boy
Even when I fear that world is closing in
It has no chance against the things that you have been
And will be
beyond me,
outside me,
on your own

Hey little one, tonight it's you and me
I'll order what you like and we'll watch the old tv
I like a long night of waking from my dreams
'Cause I lay in the quiet and it's like Christmas eve
'Cause I love to
wake to see you

Age, child! I command thee!

HIS HANDS

There were a lot of things in his touch;
sometimes the slightest whisper could hurt so much
Could feel him coming nearer
His little noises and such
And then my man
Would lay his hands on me

He might touch me the way a man should
sometimes bring me to passion that only he could
Answers some earthly need whenever he would
When my man would lay his hands on me

All the kindness and protection
The tenderness and the care
When he was happy, goodness me
But then when he was scared
Those hands, they took on a life undead
They were vicious and they were small
But big enough to keep this woman's back against the wall
Lord, I didn't ask for it
Not the love or anything else
Not the years spent in the world of a man
That only loved himself
I didn't ask for it
But god it is mine now
Those hands are in my mind and soul
But Lord, it's you and me that make their power
I will pity that beautiful man
And, Lord, I will bless his path
We were both just wounded children
in a love that, thank God, didn't last
There's a lot of things, Lord, in your touch

Sometimes your slightest whisper moves me so much
Your grace and your forgiveness
the whole world and such
When you, you lay your hands on me
Yes when you, Lord, rest your gentle hands
on me

Written for Candi Staton. Thank you, Mark.

HOW ABOUT THANK YOU

I thank god for all that he's given me
I thank earth for all that she's grown
I thank you for love that surrounds me
What to do?
Just make it our own

Share with god the yield of my actions
Share with earth the soles of my feet
Share with you the laws of attraction
And with everyone, everyone I meet

Oh and I know when I lay my head down
It's a sweet life of dreams I deserve
Yes, and I know when the suns comes again
So a new chance deserving his love

I have music here in my body
I have choice, I have freedom to choose
Bow my head in thanks and humility
And in awe at the things that he does

Oh I know
I know
I don't know a thing

Written for Candi Staton,
though I don't think
she ever heard it.
It's a good song for funerals,
emphasizing happiness.

I AM A CINEMATOGRAPHER

I am a cinematographer
And I walked away from New York City
And I walked away from everything that's good
And I walked away from everything I lean on
Just to find
it was made of wood

And I was a big old bear once
And I walked away from California
And I walked away from everything that shone
And I walked away from everything I lived for
Just to find
everything had grown

Now I am a cinematographer

If you were alone, you could walk away from Louisville

Everybody's jobs are all mixed up.
When Bresson describes his job
as something other than we
would suppose, he frees others
to look at our own work &
re-describe it. Some song-
makers might call themselves plumbers
or painters or carpenters.
I like "director of photography," in the style of James
Wong Howe or Conrad Hall.
The 'big old bear' is pure Loretta Lynn.

I AM DRINKING AGAIN

I am drinking again
I'm on my seventh cold glass of gin

Life is a tribute to you
And so is dying
And drinking in this way
To die is what I'm trying

I am drinking again
I'm on my ninth cold glass of gin

People argue with me
I have never been stronger
Nor held so strong a feeling
Inside of me longer
O but I know just what I need to live this life

And all of us here raise our eyes and our spirits
Our hands and our voices
That your ears may hear it

Candle-lit, this is a valid
daily announcement. Less
so in the age of electricity.
"It's cold gin time again."

I AM GOODBYE

You are hello,
A glowing cry.
Heaven we go,
Never say die.
I'll likely never know the answer why.
You are hello, I am goodbye.

I am goodbye
Like the end of something wonderful sometime,
Like the way that a wound-up toy top unwinds,
Like a beast in the distance you can't tell if fur or fowl,
Like the last thing you hear just before you hear the howl,
I am goodbye.
Like the absence that more and more crowds into my mind
I am goodbye.

How simple!

I AM STILL WHAT I MEANT TO BE

I am still what I meant to be
And I'm losing my mind
and our burdens must lessen
Though our enemies thrive

Crowded the hall with stock women parts
Candles were lit, burdened the hearts
Felt a bad vibe kick in just then
Things seemed to smolder, enclosing us in

Down in the basement, up in the attic
I promised you that I would not stay sick
Here is the hand now placed over the heart
Admire it lover, rend it apart

Regardless of all, I will not stay in
Off to the market I'm going again
Kicking the dust, waving at all
Covering the face, starting to bawl

I am still what I meant to be
And I'm losing my mind
But our burdens must lessen
And our enemies die

Every time I fear that
I am losing my mind,
this song reminds me that
the fear will subside
and clarity return.

I CALLED YOU BACK

And I called you back to a place beside me.

Love found us easily,
And if that's all we have
You will find
We need nothing more.

And every time we kiss,
We find ourselves in love again.

The older that we get,
We know nothing else for us is possible.

Now when I am quiet,
I hear your voice in everything.

I called you back
To a place
Beside me.

To long marriages.

I DON'T BELONG TO ANYONE

I don't belong to anyone.
There's no-one who'll take care of me.
It's kind of easy to have some fun when you don't belong to
    anyone.

Time has come to lay childish things to the dirt,
See what age brings.
If I follow the song I hear, will another come near?
For a moment I thought I had
Someone wanting to call me Dad.
Then a storm came from cloudy sky
And fire was doused from on high.

It's a truth that when sun is high,
So my feelings give love a try.
Every night when the sun descends
I start doubting again.
There's a body made just for me
Lying somewhere curled lonely.
When I come to her life one day
Will she be hidden away?

> I thought it was Merle Haggard,
> but it's Floyd Tillman.

I GAVE YOU

I gave you a child, and you didn't want it
That's the most that I have to give.
I gave you a house, and you didn't haunt it
Now where am I supposed to live?
I gave you a tree and you did not embrace it
I gave you a nightmare and you didn't chase it
I'd give you a dream and you'd only wake from it
Now I'll never go to sleep again.
I'd give you a treasure and you'd only take from it
Look at the hole where jewelry had been
Baby oh baby
Why must you escape from it,
This love that we once called our friend?

I gave you my body and you ate a-plenty
I gave you ten lives and you wasted twenty.
Now I'm standing empty, helpless and bare, without a morsel
    left of me to give
And you, you have vanished, into the air
The air in which I must live

There's times when folks are
mean & cruel because they
want to see, from outside,
what it looks like, having
already experienced cruelty
many times from the inside.

I HEARD OF A SOURCE

I heard of a source down far in the east
Forbidden, of course, to all but the least
And I heard of a spring from someone who drank
Holes in my mind, I forgot who to thank

Wash my ends!
Clean my tongue!
I don't want to go to hell anymore

My dad was a bear, my mom was a skunk
My brother exploded the thoughts that he thunk
We lived on a hill where all we could see
Was the routes and the eyes that were all closed to me

Anything can end suddenly!
I still want some love for me

Some aloneness brings with it welcome clarity.
This is from a group of ten songs
delivered as directly as possible
to their audience, so that
the stain of wondering and
the dirt of worry were
immensely lessened.

I'M DRAWING LINES

I'm drawing lines
From yours to mine
Making up for lost time
'Cause there's not that much difference
The end will come
Everyone struck dumb
Pageantry & parade
Stripped of all its significance

You don't know who a brother is
Till you've looked her in the eye
Known the voice & experience
Of who belongs beside you
Something else finally tells you
Where your final home will lie
When you finally look around
& see whose true love's inside you

I'm not singing much
You don't already know
I just hope I'm giving voice
To a song that's worth singing
Melody & harmony
Can electrify your soul
Give you all that you'll need when the judgment bells are
        ringing

I'm drawing lines
From yours to mine
Making up for lost time
Cause there's not that much difference

Written for John Legend to sing, and he did, with modifica-
tions. The recording became available on a Target-exclusive
deluxe edition of his CD. He asked me to explain where it came
from. I responded with the longest explanation I've ever given
for a song's meaning + intention. Regrettably, I've misplaced
that explanation.

I SEE A DARKNESS

Well, you're my friend
That's what you told me
And can you see what's inside of me?
Many times we've been out drinking
And many times we've shared our thoughts
Did you ever
Ever notice the kinds of thoughts I got?
Well you know I have a love
A love for everyone I know
And you know I have this drive to live I won't let go
But could you see its opposition comes rising up some times?
That its dreadful and position comes blacking in my mind
And that I see a darkness?

Well, I hope that someday, buddy,
We have peace in our lives
Together or apart
Alone or with our wives
That we can stop our whoring
And pull the smiles inside
And light it up forever
And never go to sleep
My best unbeaten brother, this isn't all I see.
O no, I see a darkness.
And did you know how much I love you
Is a hope that somehow you
You
Can save me from this darkness?

when darkness falls, only darkness has
the power.

I SEND MY LOVE TO YOU

I send my love to you.
I send my hands to you.
I send my clothes to you.
I send my nose to you.
I send my trees to you.
I send my pleas to you.
Won't you send some back to me?

Send your ways to me.
Send your call to me.
Send your days to me.
Send it all to me.
And when I'm high and square,
When I would have you there,
You will be . . .

The moon is falling.
My wounds are calling.
My head is bleeding.
And I'm a duck.
The lake is cracking.
It hears me quacking.
Fuck the land, and two if by me.

Nonsense, to bring a smile.

I TRIED TO STAY HEALTHY
FOR YOU

I tried to stay healthy for you
I stayed at that cane's length from peril
But lowly threads constrict my heart
As you perch on that barrel

Sing to them all and I'll stand by
Though jealousy it threatens
Smoke surrounds my blackened lungs
It is my only weapon

I hate these bags beneath my eyes
I know when your song's over
You'll come back to this bed of ours
And be my only lover

And carnal thoughts, they are beyond us
A man I am, but only
To be your faithful other half
That neither one be lonely

Cold and old and here today
Our faces melt together
I would I had the means to make
Our persons one together

We are you and me and so it is

It was an old Scottish melody that these words
were written to. The scene described is more
bohemian. How do older folks maintain love out
"among them"? That was a twenty-two-year-old's question.

(I WAS DRUNK AT THE) PULPIT

I was drunk at the pulpit. I knew it was wrong.
And I left in mid-sermon, tempted by a bar-house song.
The pews creaked and shifted as they turned to watch me
    leave,
And I pulled a little bottle from the pocket in my sleeve.

The sunlight was stronger to my church-dark widened eyes
Than the light which had blinded me with Christ's own
    half-lies.
Yes, mid-Sunday morning, my old playmates sat
'Round a stumble-stained table; Christopher spat
And he kicked out a chair and showed me to sit,
Then they started back singing in that shit-smelling pit.
They were grinning and dribbling with comforted heads.
Their wives were in church or at home and in beds.
Well I sucked down a cupful and God shone within
In a red earthen mask, and I saw where I'd been was a
    palace of sin.

Let them abstain on unbucking high horses;
Poor wooden structures which merely eye courses
That these log-heads run just to find some respite
In the whiskey-induced holy unending night.
Yes, I thought I saw new light, a black one which dimmed
The bleached garments with which mangled peons stayed
    rimmed.
Oh, the church songs, they paled next to this fiery chorus
Composed from a living depth especially for us.

There were arms linked and sympathy gilded the glaring
Of these bloated companions, who hid neath their swearing
Some need for another, kin to brother lust,
For which coarse words and music was faith and was trust.

Yet I saw a dependence, an inherent weakness
Within walls which hid sunlight and hindered all frankness.
That floor there supported what souls couldn't stand
On their own in their own eyes, to hint they are men
Who are slave to their vision, but to that alone.
Yes, each of them cloistered fear of being alone.

Wherever folks gather to imply a rule,
They are each one a sinner, each one a fool.
For if I drink my whiskey, and if I sing a song
I have no breast companion, a-trailing along
To imagine a sharing of burdens I earned,
To steal from the embers I strove so to burn.
God is one's corpus, and Jesus one's blood
The world is within you, without is of mud.

I remember a Christmas communion where I silently scoffed
at the priest as he administered the wine. "Do you know *who is
really* tasting this?" was racing in my mind.

I WILL WATCH WITH YOU

do what you will do
i will watch with you
though i'm charged to wait a while
i will wait for you in style
with you as a guide
i stay a while
watch with me

i won't ask you to be friends with me
nor to stand by and protect
i can't ask you to lay hands on me
just show me some respect

and in rough times
i can be with you
laying early in my bed
and in time i go to sleep
and you lay a kiss upon my head

if an end comes
it is good to be
in the presence of a few
with a few friends is how it should be
when everything is through

do what you will do

Apologies & respect,
again & forever,
to the musical artist Joe Wise.

I WON'T ASK AGAIN

When I ask who I am, I ask it just of you.
And you look at me puzzled, saying, "What am I to do?
If I don't know the one thing I need to give you help:
The simple unheard knowing of who I am myself."

I won't ask again
It would not be good
To know what only
Those who've earned it would

And then I ask you where I'll go when eyes are shut,
For one night, or one moment
or ever, ever?
but how can you let me in on secret secrets
or give me the smallest clue as to what living is for?

I won't ask again
It would not be good
To know what only
Those who've learned it would

No, I won't raise the thought
'cause quietly I'll go
where you go right with me
and quietly we maybe will just know

A dog's life.

IDEA AND DEED

What's the winter's cold negative press?
What's the spring with its air of rebirth
To those felled under wildest duress,
Trading freedom for a false sense of worth?

Let the love of our own sacred right
To the love of our people succeed
Let friendship and future unite
And flourish in idea and deed

Let the costume distinguish the strong
Place riches in lowest esteem
It's for excess that people do wrong
And to liberty honesties lean

Letting one minute go on
Without seeing yourself with an eye
That is watchful and kindly and strong
Is as letting the soul drop and die

> Dick Gaughan based a new song on a skeleton of
> words more than 250 years old. And here I saw Gaughan's as a
> skeleton anew.
> The only way forward is.

IDLE HANDS ARE
THE DEVIL'S PLAYTHINGS

Idle hands are the devil's playthings
And the devil lives deep down.
Deep down among the fiery rafters,
Eternal screamers, unsated sinners;
Those what let their souls get the best of them,
And now they live deep down.

It happens now, this endless hardness,
Overfull lifeness, troubled lostness.
It happens now in total darkness,
And now is keeping on going.

The finish comes, and it's always over.
That's the rest. The end is on you,
And you aren't there for you nor me.
Don't thank him, don't say a word.

> Why this isn't sung
> around the table as a song of grace
> at houses of the broken-minded
> worldwide is beyond me.

THE IDOL ON THE BAR

Surely there must be an idol here
Up behind the bar, some statuette
Some little femish pint forced into a painful pirouette
Whose honor we should guard
From the unchecked throat dung sailing
Let the quick-wit, thick-wit free his tongue
Leave the lower, baser minds flailing.
She would not stay straight for these wise folk
O'er a barstool she'll kindly lay
While for dolts, she'll stick petrified
Tween the register and stack of trays.
A nightingale yet to age into fluidity
An approachable voice of youthful cuteness
Which will finally send the piano's wires
To its hollowed home of muteness.
At last, the repetition of each hometown tune
Will be shed to the maiming lion, memory
To inter their intended anthemnity
Or reduce fucks to lonely seductive glamoury:
"O, I recall the dance with Lily to that very tune
when she did say I was without manly peer!
And, idol-on-the-bar, she was not unlike you,
Your queenly stance recalls her spirit here."
But this idol has no mind for the drunks' musings
Yet not without joy our princess reigns.
It is her pearlies what keeps her throned
And our gesticulation hovering twixt joy and pain.
A moment from her lips a whisper issues from
Her eyes winkle-twink and say "I love you, dear,
Pull yourself up bodily, call some strength in.
A shepherd o'er the bar to kill the wolves in here.
I can't stay here. I can't stay here. I can't stay here."

Riding a train alone overseas, men
singing in the next section, voices all
together. What were they singing? This
is what I imagined. There was an LP,
on the cover a fat Azerbaijani man,
bald & middle aged in a dark sweater,
his head leaning on his hand. The melody came from this LP.
Still & all it's Roy Bean territory.

INTENTIONAL INJURY

In time
You find
Your way to release
And then
It goes
Away again
What had been the strongest force against you
Becomes your only friend

You can't help but laugh
And I own your soul
A shadow
Unwanted
By any on earth
Most of us
Rejoice
At your awful crying
We live to force you to regret your own birth

Sky falls
Ground is gone
Our lord
Is uplifting
Your worth has dissolved
The balance of love
Is shifting

No way
To lose
There is no way to lose
Can't lose
Your way

When there is no way
We'll reify
What had been your home
And all of your power becomes ours today

Spent all this energy
purchasing tickets for
a high-flying, knuckle-
whitening ride
only to find,
at the head of the line,
a "back in 10 minutes" sign.

ISLAND BROTHERS

sing
only when you're strong
to others only all night long
and close your mouth and eyes
otherwise

my brothers gather 'round me,
they see me when I'm down,
when I can't get out of bed,
I'm tired and motive bound.
helpful or unhelpful
their words come flowing 'round
and I rally

sing only when you're strong
to others only all night long
and close your mouth and eyes otherwise

thunder is a love sound
and rain & cold are cool
some lose their houses
and others become a fool
out of older mouths
come insolence and drool

and I rally

peace be all upon
the ones buried together
no names and still recalled
as ones who died together
one is now silent
while one can love his brother
and I rally

sing
only when you're strong
to others only all night long
and close your mouth and eyes
otherwise

If you can't speak it, son,
sing it! So says Lightnin'
Hopkins in his long
spoken preamble to
the song "Mr. Charlie,"
in which a boy
can't properly
express the urgent
fact that the rolling
mill is burning
down.

IT'S TIME TO GO HOME

We wanted to see the world
Go out and speed to roam
And after these days among you
It's time to go home
When I was a little boy
O all of the world was mine
What is it to be a man?
But to know when it is time.

At home we sing to people who hear
The words we sing are listened to clearly
The sound of fire is in our ears
It's time to go home
This world ain't ours, leave it behind
It's time to go, time to go home

We came from our home to leave
Some horror of war behind us
Wherever we look, we see
Those horrors, they come to find us
Riding on pirate ships
And blowing on human bone
Blank faces and shaking hips
It's time to go, time to go home

At home we sing to people who hear
The words we sing are listened to clearly
Sound of fire is in our ears
It's time to go home
Pack our bags and clear our minds
It's time to go, time to go home

I'm a man
And you who are near me
You help me to understand
What it can mean to hear me
I'm sorry I went away, in a way
And now I'm returning
The next time I leave your side
Will be when my body's burning

At home we sing to people who hear
The words we sing are listened to clearly
The sound of love is in our ears
It's time to go home
How could we know what we would find?
It's time to go, time to go home

Written for Aliou Touré to sing with his
band Songhoy Blues.

JOLLY ONE

When you ask me to sing
It feels like my heart would burst with pride
And I look at your face and tears come to my eyes
All that's harsh and wrong in my life melts into one sweet song
And my love spreads wings like a glad bird flying over the road
I know you take pleasure in my singing
I know that only when I sing do you hear me
Because then I touch things I can't touch
I touch parts of you that I can't really touch
Then drunk with the joy of singing
I forget myself and call you my friend
I'm here to sing you songs
From this room I have a corner seat
In your world I have no work to do
My life is just to sit and sing these songs that have no purpose

Whenever I am introducing
or re-acquainting
an audience or myself
with this whole endeavor,
I start here.

129

JOLLY SIX

She who had always remained in the depth of my being
In the twilight of gleams and of glimpses
She who had never smiled
Nor given it up in the morning
Will be my last gift to you
Folded into the last song
Words have wooed her
But haven't won her
Persuasion has reached to her but come up empty
And I've gone from country to country keeping her in the core
    of my heart
And around her have risen and fallen the joy and decay of my
    life
And over my thoughts and actions,
My slumbers and dreams,
She moved but kept alone and apart
And she stayed alone in whatever you call it
Waiting for you to see her

(I found a joy of my own)

Talkin' 'bout that elusive musive
(after Tagore).

JOY AND JUBILEE

There's no reason to be seen.
No-one knows where I have been
Where I have been!
I mean love is what I mean.

Joy and jubilee!

This is what I want to be.
Everything's inside of me,
Inside of me
Where only you should be.

Joy and jubilee!

Everything
Is on the wing.
And every face is in a hidden place.

Well, just a love song is all,
with a snatch of Sunday morning ecstasy.

JOYA

God bless the chaos, I'm ready to go
Made my provisions, written my notes
Too bad the folks remain on the earth
To see me deny, no to renew my birth
And even my swallow, my sweet one of all
Will be angry and bitter and briefly withdraw
For I've done much protecting and hiding of hardness
The awful emotion I never could bear
I was always afraid to reveal what I'm knowing
Like I have a particular kind of thing growing
Indifference, a bosom ally to despair,
Soaks itself in to the skin and the hair

I keep all my cards at my chest without playing
The ones that I knew I was all this time(while?) saving
And rarely referred to it rarely gave clues
That I had this deep sickness I tried not to choose
That I had here inside of me a key to self-knowing
So base and respected, neglected and flowing(growing?)
Perversion and what might be called paranoia
Description defies though the concurrent Joya
And every corpuscle and each fold and wrinkle
Subknuckles perception of what's within my vision
And hearing distorting and feeling is lying
But it never succeeds to prevent me from trying

What a soliloquy! I heard it
sung one night by an ant
on the windowsill.

132

JUST TO SEE MY HOLLY HOME

just to see my holly home
evil jack he walks alone
swings a club and stinks something awful
well give him a painful jawful

sara walks a slinky strut
very gorgeous and anxious slut
has a love scar on her wrist
well give her our painful fist

in come babies one, two, three
like to bounce them on our knee
want to stay and grow up with us
baby stew will surely fill us

pound them down and pound them out
older ladies scream and shout
hide their bodies in the reeds
shallow bed of soil and leaves
out will grow ideas and laughter
up will rise our earthly daughter
water floods and all upon it
up upon our bloody planet

now we've ended all who'd harm us
no-one left here to alarm us
and we live just us alone
safely in our holly home

just to see my holly home
just to see my holly home
we will live just us alone
safely in our holly home

In the place of mature guidance
in the forming of a life attitude,
we may turn to dream & song,
which are, in themselves, mature
forces, dreams especially so.

KID OF HARITH

O will I be faithful to you
And never to separate now you have found me?
Or will I, regardless, be true to how you
Think that I am and know that I should be?
I watch things painted on public walls now
But I see other things, as well, behind
But right fuck in front of my spirit is how
The real road's laid out in a line
I see it lit up, headlights and lightning
While your eyes are fixed on the dark of the car
I no longer cry, I don't find it frightening
But wound up and bound up so near where you are
For how can it be to be so much with you
When there are those that totally laugh at me?
I pray so often that some fluid will pass through
While I slowly strengthen my vocabulary
It is not an urge, it is more like a duty
To begin to explore again things of the world
To re-saturate skin with injections of beauty
And to mess with, undress with some jewel
And I think you do not notice, do you?
For I am only wind and weather, only to you

> Titled to express plans for
> bridging a pretty darn vast expanse.
> The melody barely exists,
> a spring dribble.

KIDS

Kids . . . I hope in twenty years I can still sing this song.
I feel my mind is going . . . for a long time now.
I have gone from place to place,
weeks
or only steps ahead
only,
of something following.
Now I am becoming afraid to move.

When I am still,
they will recognize and terrorize one of their own.
Kids . . .
I hope in years to come
I will be strapped to the movement of time
in such a way that this still makes sense.

The fear that drove much
of this song making. Like
many/most fears, when
the future came to pass
this fear disrobed
and what was left
was something strong
enough to glory
in god's gift.

136

A KING AT NIGHT

There is grime on my face
There is crust in my eye
There is no-one in the place
But no-one said goodbye
This is how I start another day in my kingdom

There is hate in my heart
This is how my day starts
There is blood on my hands
From the murder of a man
And this is how I start another day in my kingdom

And where is my queen?
She's as gone as can be
She's a fine-looking lady
And she likes to go down on me
And I like to go down on her too

In Indya there's the Taj
On *Good Times*, there was Raj
But here-ye look and see:
All there is is me
This is how I start another day in my kingdom

There are good times to be had
Only insane is really bad
The lord and I agree:
It's not that off to be what we are . . .
As long as we're royalty.
You fuck and what's to do?
It's not your kingdom too

The joke is that
Raj was on *What's Happening!!*,
not *Good Times*. Singing this
song, the second verse always gives
me pause.

KING ME

I can't hear it play fast no more
the pace is proxy for my patience
Keep our eyelids at half-mast
Watch our friends wander through
And king me, baby

I'm no fan of you most of the time
I'd just as soon be alone, you know
In fact I'd rather be on my own
Waning in my own air
So king me, baby
Please king me, baby

Sometimes it's your smell what gets me ill
Sometimes it's your blushing laugh
When that litost (blah blah) curdles my blood
I figure you are just one big inherent mistake

Yes you have pulled my manhood into your corner
and if I can get up enough strength, enough will
To pull to your side, I want you to reach into your reserves
Top me off, tide me over, make me a man
And king me, baby
Please king me, baby
King me, baby
King me, baby

A little white Solomon Burke
teaches his own self the errors
of his stupid ways and demands,
because it is called
for, to be crowned.

KNOCKTURNE

Fire burned and blew out flowers
Showing me its comely powers
Still and all it would be hours
Before I would get burned

Someone mawed and put my cock in
Corner-eyed I saw it lock in
Twisters rolled but no-one walked in
And only love was learned

Now I truly love you wholly
No-one else could e'er have stole me
And the world so far below me
For ye and me it turned

Before there were cameras
on everything, these things
happened on the regular.
Every embrace left a permanent
stain on the household.

LAY AND LOVE

From what I've seen, you're magnificent
You fight evil with all you do
Your every act is spectacular
It makes me lay here and love you

From what I hear, you're generous
You make sunshine and glory too
When you walk in, things go luminous
It makes me lay here and love you

From what I know, you're terrified
You have mistrust running through you
Your smile is hiding something hurtful
It makes me lay here and love you

It makes me lay here and love you
I'm filled with violet and red and blue
I have a feeling from what I do
That you might lay there and love me too

This is a spell. THE LETTING GO was full of spells.

LESSONS FROM STONEY

I got screwed by the ones
Who put me in your path
"Now it's just you and me,"
I whisper, and you laugh.
Half-hearts, full mouths
I see you go on
And I go too, but not with you
I go with me

Carolina finds me
Not knowing north from west
Lessons learned from Stoney
Have suited my heart best
When I close my windows
I see you go on
And I go too, but not with you
I go with me

Not enough time to be honest
Let's hope that there's no final tally
Quietly, Stoney said he'd be
My loud and ornery ally
When you learn I'm half-woman
I see you go on
And I go too, but not with you
I go with me

Stoney Burke was a television series
in the 1960s starring Jack Lord.
It was set in the
then-modern world of rodeo.

142

LESSONS FROM WHAT'S POOR

When I go,
Follow my brother.
He's got the blood of father and mother.
And he has a spirit that's even mightier.

And if I hunger,
See that I do.
Bring me water,
Bring me food.
And fill me up with things that are true,
And very good.

And if you want to,
Touch my wrist
With the hands
That I have kissed
And hold my cuffs
So strong in your fist.

See now, watch
How it is I am;
Watch what I do,
And how I stand,
And stand down, boys,
For we are grand.
Right now we are.

I take my lessons
From what's poor.
That's what God
Has put me for.
Wealth is death,
Of that I'm sure
Farewell.

In case there is a sub sitting
in for Saint Peter, this is my
teacher's note, my letter
of introduction.

LET THE WIRES RING

Oh, one small thing . . . push your neck veins bulbous
And make those wires ring.
Now that little voice has passed, but here's a body asked to last.
Demanded by your ignorance to carry on this sapping step.
And where did I come up with you, that lets me rest so far and
    few?
But I will just commend the day your moves will court my
    corpse to stay.
Here we're sharing this boat,
One hull which threatens to crack.
We have a good thing,
Make those wires ring.

Just keep playing, darling,
keep on them keys.
The customers ain't payin' for you to rest yourself at ease.
And stop moaning those tunes.
There's no money in our ruin.
There's no rhythm in your fall.
There's nothing to dance to at all.
In dripping makeup . . .
In sloppy clothes . . .
In faded beauty . . .
In lonely throes . . .

Next break wash your pretty face and keep in mind that
    Johnny Ace
Was drunk, was fucked, was not on stage,
When he made that silly move he made.
And only afterwards did we adore him more and dole out
    money.
After, when his corpse was cool,
That hardly memorable fool,

Who shot the Christmas spirit down and lit up fame, that half-
    made clown.
It's every day
It's here at work
That money comes
and glory lurks.
Behind your eyes it hangs.
Quietly, it clangs.
With that black piano
Which we don't even own

Here we're sharing this boat.
One hull which threatens to crack.
We have a good thing.
Make those wires ring.

                                Self-destruction is pitiable
                            and, moreover, deplorable.

LET'S START A FAMILY (BLACKS)

saturday and we sleep late
usually we're up by eight
a swim it calls, a swim awaits
no work to do today
strange how you would stray
and drink and such odd things
this is what the city brings

evening calls and old folks fall
the phone is ringing down the hall
I told my friends not to call
that you were getting well
you still refuse to tell
where you'd been out so late
oh I'm in such a state

lately I'm forgotten here
isolated, feeling queer
when you were looking in the mirror
did you see the future's lines?
they march right on in time
and straight into the pool
oh so quick and cool

like 'blacks' instead of 'blues'

LIE DOWN IN THE LIGHT

When the sun welcomes us in
And the earth's protective skin
Fails and peels back face to chin
Then we start it all again

Why do you frown?
Why do you try?
Why don't you lie down
In the light?

Who's gonna hold my heart?
Who's gonna be my own own own
Who's gonna know when all is dark
That she is not alone?

Heed this word: *beware*
For my heart's ways are unclear
(and yet)
A fundamental prayer
Leaves the evil one stripped bare

Who's gonna hold my heart?
Who's gonna be my own own own
Who's gonna know when all is dark
That she is not alone?

Everybody says that it's all right to be there
Everybody says that it's all right to show
Time and again one of us falls behind
It's as if we tried to know what we can't really know

Questions are a way to pass the time.
Singsongy, like a kid by the river.
Do not expect answers from anything but time.

148

LIFE IN MUSCLE

if found, in dirt and sand
put a stone in outstretched hand
and force the fingers into fist
and kiss softly, lifeless wrist

called back by cracked lips
turn to see decaying hips
child-bearing, manly, shouting high
and lifeless, silent, once close by

it was good, it was hard
life in muscle, caked in lard
don't care how good, or what worth:
holding hand and held will go
back into the earth

may as well go fucking there
and make a new child, red and loved
with stars her blemish, wheat her hair
and death-advantaged, earning of

we are clean anyway
and it will stop hurting
ain't it grand, love
immortal flirting?
When the hand caresses you
and you deny it
knowing you
have eternity before you?

The best the undead can do
in making a song of love.

149

LIFT US UP

Lean into me, darling
Though the war in light is falling
I'm an awesome dreamer
In the mirrored light of star-far galaxy

People don't you wonder
How the lord has brought you under
in demon's light I'm dreaming
To the nakedness I'm scheming

Lifted up above the lie-lie
'Twas the wonder of my life
And the creature, form of superwolf
Will meet you eye to eye

And when I wrap around you
Ain't it wonderful I found you?
And God in all his stature
In his nakedness deserve

Oh, and I lift us up
Lift us up
Lift us up

Stitch this into linen
and hang it over
your marriage bed.

THE LION LAIR

I took road and said goodbye,
Friends go one way, I went mine.
I got lost then very quickly,
Started shaking, feeling sickly.

All alone and all around
Canyon clept above the ground.
There was treeless flat around me
and no evil came and found me.

Stars came out in midday burning,
Earth grumbled, stones were churning,
Colors red were rocks and sky
And powered glint infused the eye.

Had himself in no time at all,
Hand on shaft and gripped his ball,
Wished your mouth would come down on it,
Feel your lips sink warm upon it.

Beast and bird, they called me kin,
Bathed me and they tucked me in.
Laid down on the forest ground,
Stars above, they shone on down.

In the lion lair
Watch your own self
And take care
I am outside,
Almost one with
All the life in the lion lair.

All the things I thought were mighty.

LITTLE BLUE EYES

Little blue eyes
Why did I follow you?
Why did I snap at you?
I liked you so.
It was because I could not be you
I couldn't look at me and see you
Little blue eyes

Little blue eyes
You said my bed was warm
That you felt safe and good
While I just stared
You spread the news around
I loved another one
Instead of you
I came around, you would not see me
I held your hand, you could not see me
Little blue eyes

I needed just your soul so quietly
To hover next to me
Conditionally
But a moment's shame is too much to bear
Your eyes, your golden hair
I'm all alone

Truly I was a late bloomer.

LONG BEFORE

Long before what is black was blackened,
O, long before,
Blooms of gray made mother lovely.
Mother ain't lovely no more.

And long before the house was leaning
O, long before,
A corridor of boxwoods lined the entrance.
Boxwoods ain't there no more.

Dad burned the boxwoods,
And like to burn the house,
But one came wandering and beat daddy down.
O, long before.

Long before this road seemed knotted,
O, long before,
There was but one path, dim and cozy.
Path don't seem to be no more.

And long before you were my sister,
O, long before,
Gals in town they called me mister.
Ain't no girl call on me no more.

I'd cut the cart loosewise
Were you not my only dream.
Gave the hero his house,
He and Ma live in sin.
O, long before.

And long before you were an artwork,
O, long before,
Mama suckled you on her holy breast.
Mama's breast ain't holy no more.
Long before we shared a shortsheet,
O, long before,
I stood above you as you slept.
I don't stand above no more.

We've one little mobile,
And one filthy path,
And we'll drift along tongueless, unhappiness at last
Will last
And last . . .
Till we see fit to stand before
That virgin cunt, that sainted whore
Whose piss we have slept under,
Whose smell we have bore.
Is it her heelprint that marks our faces?
O, long before.

An incest ballad
in the style
of Sam Peckinpah.

LOVE COMES TO ME

When the numbers get so high
Of the dead, flying through the sky
Oh I don't know why love comes to me.

And when your mouth is laying ope,
Your head knocked back, you don't cope,
You're out of rings and flowers and soap . . .
Love comes to me.

Love comes to me
Love comes and all
It's my hand, my heart, my lip,
And that is all.

When the fever hits your forehead
And 'trusive mice chew up your bed
And you call on God, and God is dead . . .
Love comes to you.

Oh sugar, won't you be my only?
I'm a hard-hearted honeypot, hungry shepherd,
And I'm longing to be born for you

Love comes to you.
Love comes and all.
It's your hand, your heart, your lip,
And that is all.

In the night-time when you feel me;
And the backs of your knees, they conceal me;
And your eyeballs, they unreal me . . .
Love comes to me.

If you are endeavoring to begin a life
in songs, remember that you
are writing your future
and take great care with it.

LOVE HELD LIGHTLY

I was a love held lightly
Held and ignored unrightly
You watched me as I fell
And said "oh well,
What do I do with that thing?"

Curled in a puddle sourly
I cogitated hourly
Like a lonely villain I came
Up with a scheme:
Live my dream.

I live my dream.

To be like clouds or devils
High & free
And raining love all over thee
And then I flee
To be among the dungeons of the city
Thick love I plunge in
No self-pity
For this bonkers angel is true
Thanks to the ignorance of you

Thank you

Even more horrifying than
meeting a militant vegan is meeting
someone who claims that
he or she does not dream.

157

LOVE STREAMS

first of all let me say: love is a wave
is that what I must learn?

love is a stream that comes before what we can see
and then goes on in front of me
moving through the country

once I hoped I could only be
happy when wrecked by the sea
it twisted me, I would not try to run away
but made my heart change

you present yourself as the sea
and I fear the sea

love is a stream that sometimes flows inside of me
first it's black and then it's green
a merwolf's dream

love is a stream
ending in the sea
you are the sea
you always were

I'm not sure of it.
I'm not sure of love.
I'm not sure of me.
I'm not sure of me.
I hate this fear.
I hate fear.
I hate the sea.

love is a stream that sometimes is inside of me
first it's black and then it's blue
flowing cleanly around you

the bed was boat and you were me
the room afloat and tossed so violently
you disappeared into the scenery
and as a source and as an end
we are what we have always been

love is a stream
descendant drinking branching stream
you are the sea
you always were

love is a stream
it is not what we see
it comes from somewhere else
and it goes to somewhere else

for *Love Streams*
the motion picture,
and for Valgeir.

MADELEINE-MARY

sing a song of Madeleine-Mary
a tune that all can carry
Burly says if we don't sing
then we won't have anything

all the boys on ship set sail
and the mate was Madeleine-Mary
when her eyes did fill with tears
it was extraordinary
it was extraordinary
for we none of us could see it
for she kept herself kept below
and all her feelings private

none of us could get a glimpse
but all of us did want it
at night, above our sleeping heads
our sleeping dreams were haunted

so now my kids you'd like to hear
of one who reached and got her
well, if there was, well, I think:

he sleeps beneath the water

sing a song of Madeleine-Mary
a tune that all can carry
Burly says if we don't sing
then we won't have anything

Swashbuckle. Keep the boys in
short pants & beanies on
the edges of their seats.
Keep them coming back,
week after week, spending
their nickels.

MAJOR MARCH

Didn't I say "think on me"?
Didn't I tell you so?
Now I wonder if you ever
Wonder on my wondering o

It is two years since I've been happy
And two years since I've seen your face
Now I don't sleep and I don't want to
Yes I keep myself up just in case

'Cause I have grown my hair out longer
And I have grown my beard out too
Skin is failing, arms are frailing
But you'd still know me
Wouldn't you?

I have not friend or marching partner
Who will stand for me
And tell me of your bad behavior
Or of how our end will be

You can have another man, dear
To hold your stomach and your jaws
You and he can have a household
And love each other's minor flaws

Mine are major and they've gotten
So deep that I fear I'm rotten

I'm not sure this kind of misery
is very common anymore in the western
world. Maybe not since almost a hundred
years ago.

MAKE IT NOT AN EVIL MARK

All our hearts are stained
And every love is tainted
And over every red hole
A black door is nailed & painted
You would take colors all away
If it was in your power
And cut a hole
To mar your skin
And shit on every flower

Make it good
Make it silly
Make it lessened by the dark
Make it come
Onto her face
And make it not an evil mark

Laugh about it
We sing in a tradition
After all, it's song
It is not an action
Only the singing is deed
And the listening complicit
You'll die in the dark with me
And we'll sing for the sun's visit

I can't stop writing about singing.
All of the songs are, in part, about
being themselves sung. This one
overtly so.

MARRIAGE

Just coming in to where I store my hair
Just in the rift of gold and brown
Opening up a hole of life
A swallowing epic as we fuse

No children path-side
Though listening we hear them

So we die
Who has the blues?
Not I

Check him in another tongue
And stand him in the new way
You and me sister
Going to hang on to a bigger day
Closer to joining
Closer to death
And clear the streets for us

See if they have any water
in that house down the road
And I will wait here for you
And watch the women roll by
And if you don't come back soon
I'll pass out right here and die

And so I die
Who has the blues?
Not I

When I began to read Knut Hamsun intensely
I was glad to see that others expressed
their love as I tried to.

MASTER AND EVERYONE

You tell me you don't love me,
Well I don't love you.
You say you don't want me,
Well I don't want you

You tell me there are other
Fish in the sea
And another gathers
Roses for me

On this we will agree

You do what you want
And I will do what I want;
I'm now free
Master and everyone,
Servant of all and servant to none

And constancy in love is a joke
I'm not afraid of meeting you
I'm fickle, and I brag about it;
Neither will I cry for you.
Like a bird freed from his cage,
All night and all day I'll play and sing.

And you do what you want
And I will do what I want;
I'm now free
Master and everyone,
Servant of all and servant to none

The words here came crucially
in the mail; they were in an
opera program sent by a pen pal.
Italian folk-song lyrics, adapted
by Verdi, then translated by an
opera dramaturge, then re-sculpted
for my purposes

MAUNDERING

Maundering
I'm maundering
Evil I's just passing through

Maundering,
oh maundering
Do you know what I'm wanting to do?
I'm going to find something true

Well I never wanted to be what you wanted to see
And I wish that she would be
patient with me

Maundering,
I'm maundering
Evil is as evil do

Maundering,
just maundering
God is always showing things to you

I'm going to glorify everything good
and put right what is wrong, as I should

Time was it began
There is no plan
So I hold you in my hand till you see
only you and . . .

The lovers' feet planted firmly on the
cumulonimbi.

MAY IT ALWAYS BE

I've been with you for a very long time.
May I call you
may I call you
may I call you
mine?
And you, unknown, have been with me.
May it always
may it always
may it always be.

Please don't leave my side.
Remember I love you.
None of what I have done wrong
Was ever done against you.
If you love me and I'm weak,
Then, weaker, you must love me more.
To reinforce what's also strong,
And all the love we have in store.

By example, you've shown me that living's all right.
Stay here with me, stay here with me, stay with me tonight.
And come with me when I go into the bedroom
And we'll play bride, we'll play bride, we'll play bride and
    groom.

If you had not been born you know,
What would I, what would I be then?
I would not have strength to grow and be counted, be counted
    among men.

And in the morning, we'll wrestle and ruin our stomachs with
  coffee.
Won't we be,
won't we be,
won't we be happy?
And we will rise in anger, love and ardor.
Shining, sparkling, shimmering in love's armor.

Every song is built with the idea
that it will be repeated, again
and again and again.

MEAULNES

He came by the way that he walked

And he came by the way of a half-million murders
And he came by the way of a long list of ironies
And he came by the way of the road to Sioux City
And he came by the way of the half-breeds and lesbians

And he came by the way that he walked

And he thought it
Was in there but still wasn't happy,
He knew it was less than the way that it could be
But undaunted unshaven, an eagle in britches
He set out again to unveil the earth's riches

And he came by the way that he walked

And he came by the way that I said I was leaving,
The way that I'd take if I really was going
If I had a map, that is why I'm delaying
If it wasn't in there I'd surely be staying

And he came by the way that he walked

> First verse is Preston Sturges in its
> nonsense comedy unrelated to
> the thrust of the rest.
> And, brother, the chorus is
> a chorus is a chorus!

171

MERCILESS AND GREAT

In this building I meet other followers of your word.
In these byways I hear voices I know I've never heard.
In my mind I need to get my hands upon an end.
In my room, without you now (Lord), let my firmness bend.

Does she taste as sweet as she is to me in her love?
Can I hold her through the wicked storm I'm knowing of?
Will she fondly turn her eye to see me in my chair?
Will she come and lay her lengthy finger on my hair?

In this place I see a hundred others just like me:
Big and bold, with firm foundation, resolute and free.
Why do I fear a challenge? Why do I fear age?
It's a moment, sound and strangle, writ upon a page!

Take my hand, take my harm, and hold it to your jaw.
Wrap my head in burly cloth and stroke it with your paw.
Be forgiving, wisdom-doling, merciless and great.
Single me out from the others with whom I relate.
Though they're like-minded, keep Our hours finally Us alone.
And hold me as the fire that brought us
chars and takes us home.

> Because of the music that Emmett Kelly
> wrote for these words, for a time this
> became the most fulfilling of all songs
> to sing.

MERIDA

His head buried within the breasts of a lunatic
"(And full though aged mounds they were)"
He pretended to weep
But sighed in relief
Much to the motherly joy of her

She lifted his face from her chest with her hands
And prayed on his last-ditch desire:
"Let's take a match, to this, my husband's house
And warm ourselves in the fire!"

"At last!" he thought, "At last a chance
To vacate my dismal past!"
But the beautiful lunatic's mind was mercurial
Her fire lust did not last.
It switched to flesh lust
She stripped herself and opened her sheets to him
He spun in his shoes, gambling to lose
A-tremble, throbbing and grim

Oh!

He was not the last to quiver
As he retired to his room
For she came calling
All a-shiver, stood over him in the gloom
Her nakedness hovered and steamed in the cold
A threatening glow on her scarred corpus
"How," he thought, "has she gotten so old
And balanced this wisdom and imbalance?"

Hey!

It was in Italy, where gross
sexy fairy tales are born.

A MINOR PLACE

I've been to a minor place
and I can say I like its face
if I am gone and with no trace
I will be in a minor place

well I put the shoes in line
separate the women mine
as we do what we do fine
so victorious, so benign

only take the weather warm
and the job that does me harm
since the scars of last year's storm
rest like maggots on my arm

thank you man if for the thought
that all my loving can be bought
was wisely in your gullet caught
before my loyalty you sought

o it's not a desert, nor a web
nor a tomb where I lay dead
minor in a sound alone
yes a clear commanding tone

singing from my little point
and aching in my every joint
I thank the world it will anoint me
if I show it how I hold it

My statement of purpose.

175

MISSING ONE

I know that missing you has just begun
There's years to come
And trying to sleep tonight
Next to your kin
Is fully lovely
As I've ever been

And I wouldn't trade my life
For someone's millions
And I know you left
For a reason
And the trees and flowers
And creeks and rocks
Hold your face with every season

I know I will continue
To try and please you
And even in some ways
To try and be you
But also my fulfillment
Will be to do what I do
As you taught me to

I know that missing you
Has just begun

Love me, family!
And just sleep to all of us

In which Bonny pretends to be me,
to sing things he thought I was feeling.

MORE BROTHER RIDES

Mention of the stars reduce us back,
They, about them, have time's things hanging;
We are around near the railroad track
Checking out the thundering.
Names you call could have been ours
To call and live among them;
Friends come by and spend some hours
And then right back down to working . . .

At night, things come and half a life,
Not so silly walking,
All different clothes in the half-light
And a halting way of talking.
There really was one way to be,
Yet this is not it, we think,
To be such younger folk as we
Not leveled as we drink

We're busted up, so ragged down
And kissing and subsisting;
Our eyes glint wild and roll around
And the dog, he whines insisting.
He asks that we allow the sex
To make us unrecognizable;
That we allow slow violence
To prove us re-baptizable.

Written in the basement of my parents' house,
a good place for such nostalgic brain-checks.
One of those wildly rare moments when the
past is bigger than the present.

MOST PEOPLE

Most people are gone
Desecrated in a blur
Some people never were

My worry is gone
My friends are all gone
My mother is gone
My memory denies her

Our days to come
Can't be worried on
Can't be thought upon
Can't be dreamed

And thank you
There's no room
For disaster
In my world to come

Thank you
There's no room
For love or family
In what's to come

Thank you
I love nothing more than
The freedom to obliterate

Thank you
I know what's in store
If it brings love
Well it's come too late

Thank you
For making this easy

That's all I wanted

Somebody asked for this, said "go dark."
It was an easy space to plunge into,
an awful space to inhabit, and a grueling
climb out.

MOTHER NATURE KNEELS

Waves
Under our feet
Begin and end a talk between
A head and core so sweet.
Earth makes me tremble
And I return the favor.
I am man,
Earth,
And you may know my
Walk will never waver.

You have stuck it to us
And terrorized
From inside and above.
Some cower, intimidated,
And call this cowering love.

I don't.
I stamp and trample,
Like killing moles with heels.
And before my manmade way
Even mother nature kneels.

I have more respect for those
who say 'fuck you' to climate change
than for those who bother to deny it.

THE MOUNTAIN LOW

If I could fuck a mountain,
Lord, I would fuck a mountain
And I'd do it with a woman in the valley.

If she lives in the valley,
O, if she lives in the valley,
The mighty, mighty valley of the sun . . .

Yes, if she lives there quietly,
And goes to bed there nightly,
I'd tower over peaks and in the sky.

Well, she comes tumbling to me,
It seems every night there for me,
With a different face and legs that will not quit.

Now I'm waiting on a friend
To give me advice if I ask him
And his presence will tell me what I need to know.

I would sell my belongings
In the mountains where she's living
Just to be there when she comes every morning.

Centerfold: West Virginia.

181

MRS. WILLIAM

mrs william, where is william?
where has william go?
you know you shouldnt
come into a place like this alone.
now if youd like to sit here at my table, I'll abide.
but it isnt usually my thing to do another's bride.

I'll sell my heart, I'll sell my brain,
I'll sell my love and all my fame,
my mother, maybe, and my brother too
to raise the stake to pay for you
to get you from his side.

and then I'll watch,
keep one eye open,
halfway fearing, halfway hoping,
that blackguard boy
with handsome muscle
disturb your sleep with tiny tussle
and earn by stealing mrs william.
mrs william . . . gone again.

but with your eyes and with your aura
you'll never leave a place alone.
I have you always, the taste of us cumming.
you're part of our eternal home.

you'll make the beasties and the flora
humble and bow down.

The conceit came from Haiti, where
an awesome ensemble in Jacmel
would improvise lyrics based on the
patrons coming and going at
the café where they performed.

MY HALO, IT IS DIRTY

My halo, it is dirty
Won't you polish it fer me?
I got it all rusty
When I laid in the rain

My robes are all frayed & ragged
My glow dim and busted
My halo is dirty
It brings me such shame

You tell me I should leave them
You say that I don't need them
Why fly away to heaven
When I'm here in your arms?

Written to be danced to,
nothing in here to pull
the imagination away
from the task at hand.
Look in your partner's eyes
to see everything.

MY HOME IS THE SEA

I have often said that I would like (to) be dead
in shark's mouth
a woman swimming under
her warm breath sending thunder onto parts south
and love is stripped and frayed
and duty is delayed until next life
someone has my mind, holding it so kind
it is my wife

and my home is the sea
look not for me

my home is the sea
disaster flies upon me and I scream
we can see the house lights colored from a distance
for a party is dreamed

tumble into me
my arms enfold thee, see?
I'm a strong man

and good night, love,
my tummy is round and firm and funny
that's what I am

I am under your spell
you will have me, I reckon
and the drowning this tells
is a drowning I welcome

I know nothing and am overjoyed
I know nothing and am overjoyed
I know nothing and am overjoyed

god gave you life and thought
now it's ours to waste
I have the finest love
and the finest taste

and with the sea air in my lungs
I am home

(*you are home*)

BIG FUN.

MY LIFE'S WORK

You want to go from here to there
Where is this valley?
Take me there.
I will pull ridge to ridge
With great stone cracking
Make wondrous bridge.

Our little house can seem so small.
This morning we found no love at all.
I bust a hole in the ceiling so the light will flow
And show my lack of grace, your radiant face.
They make it worth our time on Earth.

I take this load on.
It is my life's work.
To bring you into the light
From out of the dark.

The morning cry
Now a memory,
The after-prayer,
Is all we see.

So this song becomes
The melody
Of you
As you're the song of me.

One day I will be invited
to sing in Vegas.

NEW GYPSY

It was gobbled up by everyone trying to get its taste
While I marched balking at how I had been so rudely placed
Recommended was a bar where we could feel alone
Unsurrounded, unadorned, unhappy and forlorn

Never take sick advice
From the lips of sick friends
Following the sickness takes
Its own unending end

It's the land, it is the land swept over by the light
Run with dogs and wave your arms and don't come home till
 night
Does everybody talk about another one at night?
Break a button open and let lady see the light

All the bones were slipping out, now I have brought me in
Never let the weakness slip into the trend again
One of my family has a house, she's offered me to stay
And leave the love to everyone whom obstacles waylay

Never take the advice
From the lips of sick friends
Rather take it, turn it 'round
Till it suits your own ends

You can lay me out a place, it's time I had some love
Have the ladies gather 'round and do me from above

I'll trade you this song for the right to live among you.

NEW PARTNER

There's a black-tinted sunset with the prettiest of skies
Lay back, lay back, rest your head on my thighs
There is some awful action that just breathes from my hand
Just breaths from a deed so exquisitely grand
And you were always on my mind

I would not have moved if I knew you were here
It's some special action with motives unclear
Now you'll haunt me, you'll haunt me
Til I've paid for what I've done
It's a payment which precludes the having of fun
And you were always on my mind
But ho! I've got a new partner riding with me
I've got a new partner now

Now the sun's fading faster, we're ready to go
There's a skirt in the bedroom so pleasantly low
And the loons on the moor, oh the fish in the flow
And my friends, my friends seem to whisper "hello"
We all know what we know, it's a hard swath to mow
When you think like a hermit, you forget what you know
And you were always on my mind
But ho! I've got a new partner riding with me
I've got a new partner now

Mrs. Nusbaum's credit cards.
Ideas lifted from Nirvana,
the Rolling Stones, and
Johnny Cash. The Cash
song is called "Tony,"

about rodeo friends
and the trajectory
of such bonds. My brother Ned
suggested "swath to mow" to
replace "row to hoe."
Good sense.

NEW TIBET

As boys, we fucked each other.
As men, we lie and smile.
Noble enough until the first–born child
Then: we shuck our guile.

You think we don't fight?
Birds fight, birds hate.
We fight,
Even as we reincarnate

Free us and a mess of mess will come rolling down upon you.
We are not what we should be.
We just do what we do.

If we had power
We would not fight for you,
We would crush you.
We do what we do.

We have learned to continue to look at ourselves.
We leave fear of future, love for others, and guilt
Untouched on our shelves.

We import compassion without doing a quality check.

NEW WEDDING

What I Learned From Them I Will Show You
The Inner Limits Of A New Union Of Two
Of More Than Two
Of Me And You

I Want To Do Like They Done
Those Wiry Ones
Broken Ribs And Dark Sun
The New Limits Of Pure Fun

Start With A Good Idea For A Good Thing
And Stay True To The Idea
Let All Outlines Dissolve For The Good Thing
But Hold On To That Little Seed In Your Brain

All You Know Of What's Come
Was Made Of Oil And Tit And Thumb
All You Know Of What's Old
Is Made Of The Same Things We Hold

For Thomas Campbell

192

NEW WONDER

what shall we do
what shall we do about
what shall we do about the fact

that some things
some things
are so good
that nothing can come after?

change
we shall change
and all who will not change
will be left behind

in time I try,
in time I try to
in time I try to hide the fact
that some things
some things
are so wrong
that nothing can erase them

even change
and all who will not change
will be left behind.

> Everbody hollerin' "change" except they
> don't mean themselves.

193

NIGHT NOISES

Night noises are my noises
And soiled doves are my birds
Lost mornings start my days
And questions rule my words
Hate is in the closet
(It must be somewhere out of sight)
And I drink without apology
As I go out into the night

There was a man I looked to
Last I heard, he'd sailed away
Made home down in Bogotá
But I don't think he's there today
The only one I've known
To bring me comfort, awe, and fear
All at once
While keeping tools of inspiration near

He taught me to make big thoughts small
And stay ruled by human kindness
Weakness we should palliate
And not let others foster blindness
Nobility ain't much to ask
To find coming ever clearer
If a man is to keep to task
When looking in the mirror

NO BAD NEWS

Trouble, more trouble, can you get anymore?
Slow bubble boiling on the bedroom floor
Lonely, ain't lonely, someone's calling at the door
Someone lovely, and she's bringing bad news

She clenches and she cries and she lays on the stairs
Pounding on the earth and yanking at her hairs
And showing such fear at being found unawares
To be here and be bringing bad news

Well, she's told, "Hold your buttons and look at the sky.
Someone will fix things if you let your face dry.
Keep your face near the earth and your heartbeat high,
And you may transcend the bad news."

For all: hammers and nails
For all: leaves and wind
For all: love ambitions
And enemies and friends

She shakes her face so fiercely that all her features go,
And she lays like a monkey unclothed in the snow.
And her voice it decays, and before it does she goes:
"I will never again deliver bad news."

Something bad happens and a lot of people go bad themselves,
that's how awful it is.
Turning half the heart into something hard and dark,
And she had to bring here this.

Hey little bird—hey little bird
Thank you for not letting go of me when I let go of you.

This song is about putting shit in its place every time the song gets sung.

NO GOLD DIGGER

A little cash was took off me
While I lay there comfortably.
I wouldn't move to stop her theft.
Her deft hand moved across my chest.

She stole a glance, and stole a sigh
With her eye pressed up against my eye.
The heat of her against my face,
The little dead girl, the little fish.

I heard the horns in the square play
At the end, at the end of the day.

While boys and girls did promenade
In the room I stayed with her.
I knew she wouldn't steal from me.
Yeh, she lay there, trustworthy.

No gold digger tonight with me.
She gripped me goldly, and naively.
The horns died down, and thunder cracked
As I rolled over on my back.

And she still lay just to my right
And I to her left, to her left that night.

> How good it is to be in Mexico,
> even fucked over or sick!

NO MATCH

I'm no match for honest men
I'm no match for liars
No match for those who have given up
When they are feeling tired
Can't put me up against the man
Who lets his fate just be
No match for those who love the lord
And they're no match for me

I been a long time finding out
All where I don't belong
And hard to say it's not escape
When hanging here in song
I love my dreams, god knows I do
And some of them love me
And as raging through waking life will prove
Loving dreams keeps one youthful and free

Good god guides us, bad god leaves us,
Good sea hides us, while good earth gives.
Good love FILLS us, bad love bleeds us,
Bad fire kills us; O let me live!

Honesty's a hindrance when you want to be what's true.
You can be a match for me; I'll be a match for you.

If Lal Waterson were to sing it:
The stink of port wine on your mouth
The creases in your skin
The teeth that are now falling out
The gaping holes within
The hobble and the tainted view
That was once clear to see
Well age may be a match for you
But it's no match for me
As long as I do not let song die
There'll be no match for me

If Sinatra were to sing it:
I'll stand here & shout it down
and ripple with the strain
surrounded by such violent light
showering over this wild refrain
the roll of earth, the pass of time
as bad god leaves us be.
Well age may be a match for you
But it's no match for me
As long as I do not let song die
There'll be no match for me

NO MORE RIDES

And I asked could you work it out
And I asked could you work it out
And I asked could you work it out
And I asked could you work it out
No more rides
No more rides
No more rides
No more rides
Will our friendship see another year?
Better make this profit session last
Oh, my friends, shall we shed a tear?
the pale saint is fading fast
No more rides
No more rides
No more rides
No more rides
Wrote a letter, it is always said
I'll admire but I'll stand unseen
Oh, my brother, is your lover dead?
Ever whacked-out, evergreen
No more rides
No more rides
No more rides
No more rides
And I asked could we leave it out
And I asked could we leave it out
And I asked could we leave it out
And I asked could we leave it out

Contact poison. I'm sorry.

NO MORE WORKHORSE BLUES

Many lights up today
Many lights up this way

What is this road here?
Where have I come?

I am a rich man
I am a very rich man
I have good pants on,
Stitched and stitched;
I am in stitches
I am laughing at you
I am in britches

I've written books for you
I held my own for you
Where is my tongue?

I am no more workhorse
I am no more workhorse
I am no more workhorse
I am no more workhorse

I am a racing horse
I am a grazing horse
I am your favorite horse

> Where *is* his tongue? Tied in such a mess of tangles
> it's knot funny.

NO SUCH AS WHAT I WANT

what if it didn't come back?
this is how the hard one takes it.
puts her arms up around his neck,
and squeezes gently as if to break it.

she's gonna miss everything about it,
but what's best in her is the bottom has stopped.
again again what's worse gets better
til messing with what's substantial dropped.

crazy woman misleads by staring
blankly at the wall above you.
never in a hundred times will she try to pretend
to love you, o you

you or she must convert or has done
from one to the other and into another
at the core, in a cove, in an underground berth
her coldness commends anything further.

there was a black cloud having made it go so.
so you looked at her long and hard.
and ripped her shoulders and split her back
and push her quietly forward.

now you've stuck your thumb in it, you,
so scream and groan and I'll scream too

> The spider's dude is often here, too, refusing
> the ultimate things because it is not ultimate times.

NOMADIC REVERY
(ALL AROUND)

today was one where, lost in thought,
I really feel I am
losing not an ounce of what
you see in me, my lamb

I'm glad I dream of what I dream of
today a thing was burst
if you're not with me tomorrow
that would be the worst

o all around
it's kept together moving all around

my brain it beams that it's here at all
and living, I must work
to make our lives here justified
and not let trouble lurk

instead of seeing monkeys biting
I lay on the ground
while my hectic traveling partner
wandered all around

o all around a left buttock
and all around a right
all around your every curve
I'm going to go tonight
but only hold me, hold me
all the city's on me
and all they wish to scold me
and lay their hands upon me
so only hold me, hold me

and I'll return t'you baby
I just need an evening
with someone nice to hide me

There's a lot of songs in here about
dressing up as a colleague of time in
order to equal or own her. It's
obsessive. Songs are inherently about
wrastling a few minutes away from
objectively larger forces and claiming
them as ours.

NOT FOOLING

I show you how small your world is
and it doesn't matter
it grows ever smaller

you think you've seen how high the sky
and still it rises
ever taller

you're my friends
and I walk among you
that sound in your mind
grows ever stronger
all your assumptions
are righteous nightmares
our screams together
ever longer

this is the end
I've shown you what I can do
and when I say I can walk away
I'm not fooling you

thanks for wide eyes, for smiles and for earning
for building a dream all tricked out and then burning
for fixing your eyes on my hands while I'm learning
what truly never matters

you can't screw a shadow
turn out the light
all we have shared
ends with this act tonight.

it's been real

for David Blaine

NOT MOCKED

HE:
One night as I lay on my pillow
I remembered what I had done
taken the maid to the laundry room
to have a little master fun
and here I am in wife bed with
her dreaming dumbly by
Jesus, man and me will see
Jesus, man and me will see
Jesus, man and me will see
(the) circle close before I die

be not deceived
god is not mocked
whatsoever a man soweth
that he will reap

SHE:
I touch myself a hundred times
for every time that he
lays a finger or a tongue
or prick inside of me
uber voice reminds the guilty
child within me why
mary, mom, and me will see
mary, mom, and me will see
mary, mom, and me will see
(the) circle close before I die

TOGETHER:
We keep a child out in the yard
not born to us by birth
she washes with the garden hose

and dines on worms and earth
her life is happy figment of
the love of you & I
devil, you, and me will see
devil, you and me will see
devil, god, and me will see
(the) circle close before we die

be not deceived
god is not mocked
whatsoever a man soweth
whatsoever a man soweth
whatsoever a man soweth
that he will reap

> James Hall & Mattie Moss Clark each took
> a stab at Galatians 6:7. Here it's generously iced with
> human grossness.

O HOW I ENJOY THE LIGHT

it's us i liken to a covey
a polar bear has breached a pup
the palace walls are strewn with tapestries
and the window panes are splintered and shattered
with a crumpled dog on every landing
and every stranger cowers
the dress is torn, the tone demanding
the canine's latent strength

and would her loins would yield a yelp
a beating purr to steal the time with
here's where we walk, hand in hand
o how i despise it
o how i enjoy the light
of the first morning forever
wisdom, wealth tag on like afterbirth
i will love you forever

and if i don't
and if i do
the difference exists in a fiction
the day has cooled,
the time will too
we will call upon the light

> A fresh-born calf of a song, still covered in
> placenta and with legs worthless yet
> for walking. You can tell it's gonna
> be a bull.

O LET IT BE

What's on the other side of the big-looking hill
Gather your courage, gather your free will
Go over yonder and catch you a look
At what made us get up, at what made us tremble and shook

I can live without it
I can always shout it
Let me be myself

I pick the flowers, smell like a bull
Sniff at the summer, a round nostril full
Your head disappears on over the rise
And then I seize upon the time that it buys

I can live without it
I can always shout it
O let it be so

Slip off my old clothes and into a suit
Dance all around, try to recruit
The grass to my cause, splash to your memory
Exiting finally your bestial gallery

I can live without it
I can always shout it
O let it be!

A professional human being, an amateur animal.

O LORD, ARE YOU IN NEED?

When he calls on me tonight,
Will I rise in half to greet him?
He will ask of me to think of some grounds
On which to meet him.
O Lord, are you in need?

The porch across the street is cold and dark and empty;
The window to the left holds warmth and light to tempt me.

Can one that I admire ask kneeling for my kindness?
The seamlessness I granted . . . was that due to my blindness?

Your face seems hardly that which I have pined for in the
      mirror,
Nor the visage I held up to support me in life's furor.

O Lord, can you be in need?

> When you see Jesus crying over the
> destruction of his Rihanna
> concert T-shirt at the hands of
> an overzealous coin-op dryer.

211

O PAUL

O Paul I know you feel disoriented tonight
But Paul I hope you know that we're all here and we won't let
        your sleep upset you tonight
And Paul,
Stay tight upon the couch with blankets close around your
        shoulders
So Paul
There won't be cause for you to stir

My Paul, there's something in your stomach turning sour.
What happens in your head tonight's not true.

You may get cold
You may wake up and know that we're not right by

But Paul
We all
Must sleep
So go
To sleep
goodbye

Never failed me yet. But there's one thing I know:
                    that he loves me.

OLD JERUSALEM

Trouble has caused me so much grief
I am waiting for when I can go home
Time when the room was closer than my friends
And I can get some shooting done

Then I hear a footstep on the stair
The whole thing shatters
And I scream out your name
And you come running

O it is always the same.

Time passes and the room goes dark
I expect to see your figure standing naked over me
With a mole on your neck and a wry way of holding wide
The spirit of my darkened past

Then we mingle our limbs
O I hear her all calling
When we swim and we buckle
And I emote
It is the only time to catch it so
So we may as well rest and let it go

We gonna be re-joined and the children will love it
All my brothers and my sisters resting holy above it
Let us wallow, let us play, this is our god's day
Let us wallow, let us play, this is our god's day

                              Deep love, deep horror.

ONE WITH THE BIRDS

"leave me alone" is all that I say
when I have nothing in me to give away
a purple martin in her house, she hollers at me:
"why be inhuman? why be like me?"

like so many robins, like so many doves
like so many lovebirds with so many loves
like the songs of the bobwhite
without any words
when we are inhuman
we're one with the birds

at six in the morning,
you rise from the pillow
stand steaming above me; I slumber below
I'm one with the blanket
laying fragrant and loose
you're one with a whip-poor-will,
you're one with a goose

so sing with me and widely spread
your roseate wings: embrace my head
fly with me 'til we are dead
and one with the birds

like so many seagulls
like so many hawks
like so many thrushes
and so many cocks
a swallow will tell you without using
misleading
heart-rending words:
"when we are inhuman

we're one with the birds"
yes, when we hide our feelings
we may as well fly away

It's a good thing you can't hear the melody.
The muses were having
a laugh at me.

ONLY SOMEONE RUNNING

Only someone running would run right into me
Unless that someone was someone free like me

There are things I would not do
I would even be mean and cruel
And I will not stay with you
Unless you give me all of yourself

When I was a sandy blue
In friendship dwell
in western true
Smoke and pill and lovely too
That was before you gave of you

Make a future dream be ours
Through your eyes I swallow flowers
And disdain the winter showers
Choosing then to bathe in you

I sing evil, I sing good
I sing as a seagull should
And if you melted
then I would
Melt myself all into you

Can you love the one that God does?
Can you love the lily of the field?
Can you tend the soil inside her
Till all has been revealed?

Look around. Gather, gather.
Listen around. Gather, gather.
Voilà. Roy Orbison & Jean Ritchie
have a baby.

OPEN YOUR HEART

I know I lied
But I never said
That I wouldn't try
To mess with your head
I never wanted to be
So far away
I only wish you
Could hear me when I say

Open your heart
Let this snake in
Don't fall apart
Before he tries
It's not that hard
To do it again
Open your heart
Just this last time

If you didn't know
Another was there
Maybe you'd grow
To learn not to care
But as it is
There's just no hiding
It's not worth having
Who can't be abiding

Of things that I need
And things that I value
And others unknowing
Of what we go through

Growing up, I had the great fortune to have a strong, creative male friend with whom I could listen to, and talk about, the popular recording star Madonna.

OUT OF MIND

What was I saying? Where do I stand?
Is that my voice praying? Am I still a man?
I went to the doctor. She denied all my claims.
Where am I going? What is my name?
Nobody answers or looks in my eye.
You're out of my mind and now so am I.

Where is my money? Where can I sleep?
My brain just keeps boiling with thoughts I can't keep.
Why's the world keep on shifting? It's a place I don't know.
My consciousness drifting with nowhere to go.

The keys in my pocket don't open a thing.
Of having no purpose they've crowned me the king.

If I pretend that I'm sane maybe I will become so.
If I pretend that I'm happy maybe that's where I'll go.
If I pretend we're together life can show us this union.
If we love one another heaven will be ours soon.

Nobody answers or looks in my eye. You're out of my mind and
now so am I.

My friend Joan wrote a song saying
something along the lines of "If you are
going crazy, can I come along." This
was closer to where my head was, or, rather, wasn't.

OUTLAWS

My friend Lil Mattie is a real bad man
He causes trouble any time he can
Men's lives are wasted all over the land
When Mattie takes a stand

My cousin Christian has an axe to grind
He lost his baby and he lost his mind
His walk through life leaves blood and bone behind
There's no-one of his kind

It's on our skin
It's tattooed in
Don't come too close or we'll end you, friend

My woman Elsa has a heart so cruel
She killed her sister in a bare-handed duel
She met a grizzly and she took that beast to school
My baby ain't no fool

They say we're family
Well that ain't right
It's just we're all marked:
Outlaws for life

It's what we do
We're not like you
Outlaws!
Whoop-de-doo

This "Outlaw" number was
conceived to be
subliminally implanted into
the still-forming minds of
millions of adolescent boys. Alas, it was
not to be!

(THOU WITHOUT) PARTNER

Nighttime's the right time to pull all the dimes from
    your pocket
Nighttime's the right time to climb on the rocket
Nighttime's the right time to pull your shoulder out of
    its socket
Nighttime's the right time to learn a new language

Cosmonauts flying, cosmonauts dying

You picked a fine time to tell me it was time to find me
    a new wife
You picked a fine way to tell me that today would be
    the last day
When is the first day you'll repay the money that you owe me?
A sisterly severance, a cutting of cookies, adios fraternos

When will she run to me?
When will she come to me?
O buenos días
O buenas noches

No mercy you have shown me.
How could a woman with so much to live for have so many
    children?
When time came to call names she bolted and left me an
    unlabeled burden
I'm bound to my time like cukes to a new brine, or brawn to an
    old one
Besides I have no time to explain how I have been feeling

Cosmonauts flying, cosmonauts dying
Astronauts starving, astronauts leaving
No more hospitality, no more hospitals at all

When was the first time you realized the next time would be
    the last time?

> Bryan Rich came up with the cosmonauts, the mercy,
> the hospitals, the hospitality. We were in Russia.
> Bryan kept his cash in the freezer.

PARTY WITH MARTY (THE ABSTRACT BLUES)

Now my brother's disappeared and the fish ain't biting like they
    used to
And my motel room opens to a well-trimmed lawn
But the evening's warm and I know just what I'm gonna do
I'm gonna drink and party with my friend Marty
Til the abstract blues are gone
Well the cooler's full of ice and we've wedged open the motel
    room door
And there's a pair of girls just out of this world in room 104
They're on their way over with bikini tops and cut-off jeans
We don't know their names but there's no mistaking what their
    manner means

Me and Marty and the girls, we party on the ocean side
Turned off the world for a while, let the problems slide
There's no better bruise for the abstract blues than a
    K.O. to ennui
And we'll be punching the lights out until the night's out
The girls and Marty and me

Lori is an Asian American; I love the exotic type
She says she's searching the whole world for surfing the
    perfect pipe
She don't like her parents, but ain't that inherent for a
    healthy girl?
I don't know where she's been, but tonight I will hang ten
    on a surfer girl

Marty's got Susie by his side, they're dancing to a Latin beat
She's got cute little anklets resting just over her tan little feet
I can't hear what they're saying but I can tell that they're
    praying that the song won't end
And neither this situation before we all go back to that real
    world again

then in the morning, sunshine comes warning through the
    window blind
I'm laying with Lori, who's just laid with me and it blows
    my mind
And I'm thinking that this time I won't be going back to my
    former life
I'm throwing my lot in 'cause I'm glad now I've got into the
    maritime life

Me and Marty and the girls, we party on the ocean side
Turned off the world for a while, let the problems slide
There's no better bruise for the abstract blues than a
    K.O. to ennui
We're gonna get the decision, a festive collision
The girls and Marty and me

> Marty surfed down the interstates on hoods of cars.
>   I could never keep up with him.

225

PATIENCE

I wasn't born a fisherman
and I wasn't born a schoolgirl
and I wasn't born a tree of leaves
and I wasn't born o lordy lord
'cause I was a bold and tireless worker

and I wasn't born an indian
and I wasn't born arabian
and I wasn't born a man with a dream to just let it falter

and I wasn't born o! a well digger
and I wasn't born o! a fleshy thing
and I wasn't born a thing to be scorned
a thing to be ignored

and I wasn't born o! to tell the truth
and I wasn't born o! to sleep with ruth

we're miles apart
and I have no heart for weeks between coupling
well, I could bide my time with girls that live in town
with those who seem always to be hanging around
but it would not seem right to pass the night
with one not my true love

and I will align myself with nothing
and I will join my heart with no-one's
'cause I was untried
when I was applied the light of birth

The pursuit of patience is
unending. The reward of the
labor includes joyful encounter with identity.
I know where I'm going!

POOR SHELTER

If I lived in a poor shelter
I will give something back

Child will know I'm a small thing
In a thick wind blowing back

Some will know when a small limb
Comes to grow in upon the path:
Animas in a moment of sharing look back

> Stop. You have been crushed
> before your first breath.
> You have died of malnutrition
> without a Social Security number.
> You cannot speak and will never be known
> by anyone.

PULL YOUR EYES OUT, MOLLY

Be my voice and fill my eye
Sing my song and crack the sky
And unlike any other song
This one must be all life long

We don't need answers laid before us
We try to set example right
So drop your bags and join the chorus
And fill the awful night with light

The more that we can band together
The less there'll be that we can't see
And no one who lives in your heart
Could ever be an enemy

Repetition makes us holy
There are two directions, straight and round
God is time and that's my story
Thank god the ending has been found

I will pull your eyes out, Molly
I will make you strong and clean
Wait until the fire shines, Molly
The warmest end you've ever seen

> Anyone who speaks with assurance
> about the best way to live
> ought to have his tongue cut out.

PUNK ROCK

It's time to go baby
I'm loving up my shoes
A very grateful travel
And a buttery pie
But she looks kind of angry
And she turns kind of red
And she still kind of trusts me
Even after what I said:
"It's called hard luck baby
It's called punk rock
Wake up and smell the coffee
Take a sip."

A peanut butter & jelly sandwich of a song.

PUSHKIN

God is the answer
God lies within

And you can't say
that I didn't learn from you
and you can't say
that I had much to learn from you

God is the answer
God lies within

And I will not
have a good time
but leave me just the same
the statue marks the place here
where Pushkin stook his claim

God is the answer
God lies within

And I guess that
she couldn't tell me
because she found it
very frightening
and though a lead slug
would have felled me
Pushkin
rides the lightning

I can't tell you what a relief it was,
for a number of years, to sing this
song. The choruses acted as
well-drill bits and the verses gave
shape to gushers. I was brought
up excluded from "God" and was
finding my way.

QUAIL AND DUMPLINGS

Holes in our ceiling
We got holes in our roof
Hope that we got it made
now gone in a poof
When's it gonna be turn in the tide?
When we gonna see that we got God on our side?

Too big our slippers
Too small our bed
Too bent our bosom
And too broke our head
We must hit the bottom
In order to rise
Find peace in a hovel
To find home in the sky

And she says:
"What are we eating? And why ain't it grand?
Ain't I a woman? Ain't you a man?
Why wait for someday? Why make a plan?
Fuck birds in the bushes!
Let's take 'em in hand!"

Weather ain't judgment
& money ain't love.
the crimes of a criminal
ain't been dealt from above
I'll hold your hand
& we'll say it's enough
to have satisfied minds
and clean hearts and clean tongues

Quail & dumplings
Now to the end
God and her minions
As our bosom friends
We got empty tummies
But won't always be
One day it's gonna be quail and dumplings for we!

Quail & dumplings is a reasonably unattainable dish.
This couple fully knows that their dreams of succeeding to
contentment may not really come to pass. A few years ago,
chef Josh Lehman mortalized this dish at the Holy
Grale, and, upon eating it, I thought I had imagined well a meal
of fantastic proportion.

RAINING IN DARLING

darling
I can stay awake all night
but I would make mistakes, alright
'cause the body asks so much

sweet thing
I give you what I reach
taken what I had to teach
and re-rendered it with such
with such
with such . . .

o, it don't rain anymore!
I go outdoors
where it's fun to be
and I know you love me
I know you do!

> So strong a love gurgling in
> the stomach that even
> the regurge is something beautiful.

RICH WIFE FULL OF HAPPINESS

all and all is one thing today
one good effort made on its way
to take in a love and pass on a feeling
of heart in chest slowly unpeeling

Lily can take it with a smile and not a frown
in the room where she lives, blessed I guess
she wears my favor and shows it around
and in doing so, I too get blessed

rules explode and we call her mine
and she has my baby and things are fine
she can't hold her eyes still or her voice
the way nooses hold necks still in excellent poise

a jug holds a gallon and you hold my arm
and I hold a million in bottle and yarn
and gem isn't sacred where mother has breathed
you know; you told me that.

a shark and a dog, now you're laughing
the dog licks the shark dry in your photographing
and I lick you dry until you're laughing
my finger is in your behind

I woke up fat and almost unhappy
but the bigger the laugh the bigger the belly
and I bellow out and the whole bed it shakes
and you smile at my laugh as it rocks you awake

Charlie Rich.

235

RIDER

High high all night now
My eyes bugged out and I'm down on the couch
Lady's got a box pressed into my face
And a belt of beads draped around her waist

I flex my neck and lose my sight
See the stars dropping out alright
Clouds and nebulae making noises
And constellations in erotic poises

Cold in space and fingers long
Between the ears a synapse is wrong
Clicked apart and's all it can be
The last, the last you'll see of the leaves

Don't do it.
Don't go there.
You don't want to see it?
Close your eyes, stay home.

RIDING

Where you going riding, boy?
I'm going to ride on down to see you.
Where you going riding, boy,
All dressed up and with that look of joy?
I'm going to ride on down to see you.

Who you going to ride with, boy?
I'm going to bring my sister, Lisa.
Who you going to ride with, boy,
All dressed up and with that look of joy?
I'm going to bring my sister, Lisa.

Because I love my sister Lisa most of all.

Don't you know that's sinful, boy?
God is what I make of him.
I'm long since dead and I live in hell.
She's the only girl that I love well.
We were raised together, and together we fell.
And: God is what I make of him.

I've left off the coda, which came
from Joe Wise's "All I Am I Give to You."

ROYAL QUIET DELUXE

I-64 goes from someplace bad
To someplace better
Better 'cause it's far
Far away from where I met her
And because it's unknown

Life is worth nothing
All of my love is in a hole
And is dead
There is no heaven for love
It simply dies

The hills of West Virginia
Offer respite for my eyes
But like Utah, and all things lovely
The loveliness is lies

We learn that she who screams the loudest
Makes he who fears most run
And who is ruled by fear
Is oft ignored by fun

Still there is
A way to be
If we die many times
Then let death come to me

This is the last song of its kind.
Now you can be.
Now you can be all that all your weakest love can find
Ain't it the best?
Ain't it the best?

There are things that need to be
sung just once, to be true &
expressed for a few minutes and
then left to
become part of the dirt again.

RUBY
(THE COLOR OF MY DREAMS IF I HAD DREAMS)

it isn't always i am well
for sometimes i am ailing
and yet in steaming night i smile
to downplay this my failing
and make a noise to bury all
of your weeping and your wailing
and then in bed by little light
and closed off from it all
i must try and bring a conscious end to night
and hope that dreams begin to fall

the color of my dreams, they would be you . . . ruby
o if i could close my eyes and bring you to me
push your head into
make you not you not you not you
but me

can it be that my love hurts you?
O to spread you
Paw into you
Make you just a limb of what's me

and then in dreams i wander free
and see some things i'm meant to see
and sometimes even i see thee

and would the night go on and on
and not tomorrow end at dawn
and whatever mat i lay upon
dissolve

the color of my dreams, if i had dreams, they would be you . . .
    ruby
everything i do is done to bring you closer to me
when you sleep your breath it blows right through me

Can it be that you're not happy?
So sorry if creeping in to see you somehow violates you
And if, in so violating, something in me learns to hate you
There's nothing to keep me from becoming what most horrifies
    you

and illness be or wellness thrive,

my dream proves i am yet alive

The freedom to express anger.
These words were assembled
for an industrial/goth audience.

241

RUDY FOOLISH

Well, a foolish day is a foolish day
in a beautiful way
she's a panther girl
trying to steal my world away
i'm sorry when you're ill
and under the bed
and i know you will never be dead
never be dead

well a rudy day is a rudy day
in a beautiful way
she's a panther girl
trying to steal my world away

i'm sorry when you're ill
and under the bed
and i know that you will
never be dead
never be dead

Never did like cats.

SAILOR'S GRAVE A SEA OF SHEEP

Once in a while I can't stifle a smile
Even now that things come to a closing
My intentions were pure even when, I am sure
They seemed riddled with evil imposing
A marvel of time, all the visions of mine
Look to you to be past or be battered
There are those that are here, do you see them? They share
What is all that eventually mattered

you were mine and I recognize
that I couldn't be what I am
without the power of your heart and your eyes
urging me out of my jam
When you came to me you were magic, you see
You were splendid, your love was an omen
I held you inside, when we conquered I cried:
"Here is all that I need in this moment!"

It's okay it's okay
You can say I've had my day
My god and I
Don't see it that way

I was alone and my power had shown
Me to be neither worm nor master
One never sees how an untaken sea
When once entered can change us much faster
remember when you knew all things
and wanted to own your own end?
you've pushed me, you see, like a boat from a quay
and I'm off and I know where I've been

It's okay it's okay
This is done, let it be so
And now you can
Let me go

> Showing a respect not shown
> to him, the Black Captain (my hero)
> takes a moment (he has many)
> to respond to his erstwhile
> second.

THE SEEDLING

I go out back to look up at her
Smiling unluckily at my red fur
And into my own I meld my nose
My full-sized child is fully unclothed

Birdies say I got no children, birdies never know
In my hidden life I've made a seedling grow

When it is cold I shelter her in
The wazimy warmth of the monkey skin
And into my own I fold my head
My full-sized child with full-sized spread

Birdies say I got no children, birdies never know
In my hidden life I've made a seedling grow

Hawks and doves and power fists
Black hand gripping our kids' wrists
Lanterns and arrows and little monk fish
They grant my every child wish

OUTLINING SOME OF THE DARKER OF THE HERO'S
PRIVILEGES.

SHEEP

born in sheep's blood, plain and simple
washed out of my mother's temple
all around i heard them laughing
as father sheep had stood there calving
black they were, with white eyes gleaming
right in heaven, life was seeming
brittle wind blew snow upon me
i got blanketed all white and frosty
in my time i grew and killed them
or out of memory i willed them
and willed in a greater history
out of massacre and mystery
was no longer wealthy, woolly
nor anything i could grasp fully
someone rush to re-inject me
gods of gods won't you protect me?
fixed my face and marching onward
marching, running ever forward
buildings were a bloody vessel
edging me below the trestle
there in coal and whitened gravel
i built a shield of wooden baffle
inside of which i raised a fire
so i could tonight retire

everyone will tell you it's evil to be
a free-thinking pecker like bonny old me
but i'll flex my armies and blow out my gut
and prove i'll be loved by any old slut
look here in my wallet, it's loaded and true
and now we can leave here
and go and find you

Would that children's Christmas specials could grow with us. As we are allowed or forced to welcome drudgery, and death, we should be allowed our Puffs to get bigger, stronger, wilder, more inconsistent. Even our dogs die too soon.

SIXTY-ONE

I don't know why I was given life!
I assume it was to find
An abundance of love and money.
And the things that make me feel
Like this pursuit is really real
Are flirtation and alcohol.

Laying in a field of bubbles blown by lips
That I wish were always mine,
Giving pass to all my troubles,
Green mountain juju
And lovers' lack of time.

For an hour I was happy.
I was happy . . .
I was happy!
And then it all
Went black.

Watch me as I cave to what you need.
I take you in, and all that I can see
Is your world, and I try to make it mine.
Impossible, and anyway we're out of time.

Drowning in a glass of bubbles
With just a bit of wine.
Giving pass to all my troubles,
Intoxing juju
Destroying sense of time.

For an hour I was happy.
I was happy.
I was happy.
And then it all
Went black.

> Preamble. Verse. Chorus. Bridge.
> Happiness slapped together is bound to
> crumble.

SO EVERYONE

HIM:
I know my way around the world
It's a circle and it starts and ends
I've found my hands on mountain girl
And my efforts condoned by friends

HER:
I sit in my window looking out
And watch for boys lit by the moon
I have a little magic left in me
And how to make a one like you swoon

TOGETHER:
O take it, o take me,
O take it so easy
O make it, o make me
O kneel down and please me
O lady, o boy
Show how you want me
And do it so everyone sees me

We have a new leaf to show the world
Glad we do
We had to come upon it
Seems we put our money down
On black and even
And the new leaf, well we won it

Now I want the world to see
Everybody look at me
I'm a good person, and free
And you love me

Big heavy blocks, happy blocks,
two sides of an arch competing
to reach the pinnacle of
each other's happiness.
Grassroots erotic.

SO FAR AND HERE WE ARE

O once I had a partner but now that is done.
I made awful actions that I thought were fun.
Here years have come on and I live like a king,
A monarch who rules over all that he sings.
I started in old world, have come now to new.
But actions, behaviors, beliefs have come with me too.
There had been a time when the world knew my name . . .
They may know it somewhere still but I ain't the same.
I bow to the word and not to the one.
The word is the heart, is the throat, is the sum.
There's no rest for the wicked, and less for the good.
No fear for us mongrels who do what we should.

They pointed to the sky and they said it would fall.
I ended her, ended him, ended it all.
These are my conclusions from under the sun.
O once I had a partner, but now that is done.

Written to the rhythm of a Bahamian sea song.

SOMEONE COMING THROUGH

Below us he walks,
who we have waited for,
rags and dogs in his way.
Clear the way!
There is someone coming through!

He looks up at us;
we hide behind the rocks.
It will be days before we see him again.
In these days he's known to sit in a darkened room,
pained by what he's seen we have done.
Out the door and into the streets
his mind is very clear and he calls us.
It is now for us to do everything
he tells us to do,
now (that) we have lives.

"He" is singing "The Lion Lair" (page 151).

253

SONG FOR DOCTORS WITHOUT BORDERS

Well the boys in their jeans
A fire burns spleens
And I wouldn't have made it home
And one parent's found
While the other is drowned
And I wouldn't have made it home

No I wouldn't have made it home
Stuck in lamplight all alone
Yes I wouldn't have made it home
So I stayed
Traveling on my own

In a village I saw a bloody gun drawn
And I wouldn't have made it home
I lay in the ground
Fearing I'm found
And I wouldn't have made it home

Lord I wouldn't have made it home
Without David to guide me along
No I wouldn't have made it home
Just a lost creature screaming in a song

There's a new demon now
Creeping around
And I wouldn't have made it home
With his arm 'round your back
He makes to attack
And I wouldn't have made it home

David is Tibet and Berman.

SONG FOR JOHN AND ALMA

What will we do?
What will we do?
Life isn't true
Except for you
Except for when it comes to you

Brick by brick
We'll make it stick
Song by song
All night long

Where will we go?
        We'll be eating stumble pie
Leave Mexico.
        A generous portion, you & I
See our silhouette?
        Now we're heading for a fall
That's as real as it gets.
That's as real . . .

                        A daughter sings to her father;
                        A father sings to his daughter:
                                Blood unison.

                        Made for the motion picture *Edén*.

255

THE SOUNDS ARE ALWAYS BEGGING

Wild guitars came from forests
plainly, woodsmen share a calling
Flailing noises form a chorus
harmonies of arbors falling

And they "play," say Conway
and "ring," my girls sing
and plead and beg
and plead and beg
and plead and beg
and plead and beg to be heard and had and carried on . . .
Without us, song is nothing!

My wife turned crazy on me one day
Started chopping up the bed
Looked past me with gaping eyes
Left me too hard to be scared
She left, but circled the yard
All night she haunted the home
The kids went crazy, life was hard
The sounds of rings, boom

I taught the children to play piano
singing with sweet voice
Music kept their mom away
Melody fostered choice
And choice brought us these days we have
And choice brought us to our rejoicing
Always choose the noise of music . . .
always end the day in singing!

And they play, don't they?
And ring, and everything!
And bounce and boil
and bounce and boil
bounce and boil,
and plead and beg
to be heard and had
and carried on.
Without us, song is nothing!

Teach a kid to sing.

SOUTHSIDE OF THE WORLD

Where were the rapists when I was a child?
They were my neighbors (that's why I'm so wild).
Where were the drunkards that shot with their guns
And closed their shops early so we could have fun?
Where were the women who spread the disease?
Who spread love so freely, and so spread their knees?
They went to the southside to make their own laws
Away from the knawing of innocent jaws.
Lord, they went to the southside, and we must go too.
If we want our freedom, that's what we must do.
If we want happy families, that's what we must do.
Give me donkey ears! Give me honky tears!
Give me black blood, and that of queers,
To mix with my own!

Come with me to the southside where we'll make our home.

> I didn't know how to follow
> Donald O'Connor's advice,
> "Make 'Em Laugh," until
> this song came along.

THE SPIDER'S DUDE IS
OFTEN THERE

I love to see a milky white angel
Getting her deserved rest.
Drooling into my chest hair
And softly scenting our love nest.
We held each other up
On the bobbing streets to home.
She humored my softness, recognizing good intentions.
I'll let your spider eat my fly
If I can scratch your belly.
And never let me catch you with another
Unless to teach me a lesson.

Sweetheart you couldn't do better
I eat mush like a ramrod
I got a whale of a wild heart
Now

If heaven's tits weren't gleaming up to tease me
I'd tumble down the basement stairs.
To live amongst the dog beds and the pipe-ends
And eavesdrop when you slip into the tub.
You'll howl with all your doors closed, as you watch me
    stumble past
A golden-gilded stumbleweed, a husband that will last.

> Hey daddy-o. I don't want to go
> down to the basement.

THE SPOTTED PIG

Hidden in the chest
At the foot of my bed
Is the filthy spotted pig
I've owned for so long
You've heard its noises
And cried while I slept
Thinking that you wailing
Resembles the spotted pig's song

Your modesty I love
Your beauty I cherish
Your fear of death I envy
Your vanity I punish
Humility I welcome
For to live with the pig
You should have no pride

Little hairs from your swimsuit
Sprouting from the sty
Where can I put my fingers
That will make you weep?
Tonight with windows open
My little beast and I
Will betray our watch
And disturb your sleep

It begins & you are nodding, smiling,
humming along. Then your face reddens,
darkens, & you turn away, pretending
not to know me, desperate to forget
the whole thing.

STABLEMATE

How could one ever think anything's permanent?
How can you sleep when I'm going away?
I haven't a reason left in my head
To not go away.

Haven't you heard I've a new invitation?
To give to a woman who sits and who works,
Whose father does not ever not let her have
Something she wants.

When will you work and when will you struggle
To die in a day and rescind your own fate?
'Cause I haven't the time nor have I the need
To sit here and wait.

It took her in when it just didn't want to.
When she came to the house and she sat in the yard
And she whistled and stared at the day make its way.
It was found to be hard.

It was hard to know you were the only lover
But that you would test it so carelessly.
That you would ruin me if I would not have you.
This is your way.

To invoke an un-played trumpet.

STRANGE FORM OF LIFE

A strange form of life kicking through windows,
Rolling on yards
Hitting in loved ones, triggering odds
A strange one

And a hard way to come into a cabin,
Into the weather
Into a path walking together
A hard one

And the softest lips ever,
twenty-five years of waiting to kiss them
Smiling and waiting to bend down and kiss twice
The softest lips

And a dark little room across the nation,
you found myself racing
Forgetting the strange and the hard and the soft kiss
In the dark room

And a strange form of life kicking through windows,
rolling on yards
Hitting in loved ones,
Triggering odds
A strange one

Kentucky fado.

262

A SUCKER'S EVENING

I will not pick a fight with you
I'd be scared I'd foul it up
What with one of your arms
I could get busted up

Don't come around here angry
This is a house of water
You'll be cold and soaking wet
'Ere you leave here

Make a noise, crack a glass
I'll hold his arms, you fuck him
Fuck him with something
The fuck—he deserves it

Stay here while I get a curse
To give him a goat head
Make him watch me take his place
Night has brought him something worse

Lady and I, we like to have our times
Tonight we spent ourselves
We ran it dry like sand
We had all there was to spend

> More armchair perpetration, in the writing.
> In the singing, it's the seed of something else.
> How can I keep from singing?

THE SUN HIGHLIGHTS
THE LACK IN EACH

condition is uncertain and likely to go
I sit like I did; like I may always
under capsized boats, discouraged
to know how sunk can be days
struck under, blown out, to cause busts
I can remember, thanks to the smells
how colors can be, and how to smuggle in breath
to a column or corridor hemmed in with death

o my
our friends all within reach
and
the sun highlights the lack in each

with enough money a woman is mine
and I hers, to challenge and throw her over
over the rail, over a bedpost, out in line
watched by whatever can spring from her
ain't it always watched and lined out by it?
we can describe it, or shoot it, here we go
take me for a ride, blindfold it, forget it
I will be back in the smells you know

o my
our friends all within reach
and the sun highlights the lack in each

with luck, I'll come up near the other
who mocks me, all gruff and full and ugly:
"a small soul, perhaps, but burning brightly,
and guttering on my things like a wave"

We use the ugly & broken as tools
building our lives up until
they are undeniably ugly and
broken. Then a repellent circle
of fear surrounds us, eventually
dissolves, and we become tools.

TAKE HOWEVER LONG
YOU WANT

take however long you want
I will be here when you haunt
you can wait here forever
by the trees alone
and I won't be sorry when you're gone

take however long you need
as times will wait around to be
something tall and black and glamorous
like about what you would dream
but you won't be hanging 'round with me

when you're about to go away
lie when they look you in the face
laugh and make jokes
like the others do
and at night I will be hanging out with you

I will be here
when you need to leave
and I won't be sorry when you go

A bitch to comprehend,
a joy to sing.

TEACH ME TO BEAR YOU

You wrote your name on a paper and gave it to me;
for years in my pocket where no one could see.
How can I change the way that I felt?
I slipped the paper in the pocket of somebody else.

Won't you teach me to bear you?

Someone with matches; someone with bronze;
someone with blue eyes
to gaze upon
your name, your whole story, your whole life to see.
The story you had given to me.

Won't you teach me to bear you?

I want to read you a life of parties and wisdom,
of care and explosions and wild summer eves . . .
but my hands are empty, and my throat cracked and drawn,
because I gave away the name you gave to me.

Yes I sang away the name you gave to me.

> Teach me teach me teach me.
> School should teach
> us to bear each other.
> If you can't bear it, sing it.

THAT'S WHAT OUR LOVE IS

Don't go to bed
if you know that something's waiting
to grab you in the night and throttle hope from your heart.
Don't close your eyes
if the ills are fornicating and conceiving of an evil to break you
     from the start.

No, STAY and play with ME.
We'll lock it down and sleep outside, our heads on shoulders.
Okay? That's how it BE;
that's what our love is,
and will hold us til we're older.

Don't go indoors if the walls that are waiting
have a way of hindering healing laughter in your chest.
And don't try to speak
any words of how you're hating
when the song of how you're loving is always best.

No, STAY and play with ME.
We'll lock it down and sleep outside, our heads on shoulders.
Okay? That's how it BE;
that's what our love is,
and will hold us til we're older.

I believe these are end times.
Wouldn't it be best to be together then?
The smell of your box on my mustache or a crossword on our
     mind.

The words were tribute to smooth country
music circa 1980 + then Emmett brought
in smooth pop music from the same period for
the music.
"It doesn't get any smoother" (overheard at a Don Williams
show).

THEN THE LETTING GO

There was someone a long time ago
(*Come follow me here and then we'll go*)
Who played with me whenever it snowed
(*To a fortress in the snow*)
She lived nearby and I'd walk her home
(*On these bushes berries grow*)
Then I would go to my own house alone

Then one December bad weather came on
(*We will eat them seeds and all*)
I went to our shared place and nobody came
(*Hand in my hand, nose and nose*)
And it was dark before I made my way home
(*Shall we marry or shall we go*)
And sat at my window and watched the snow come

When I had children I asked them to stay—
When the weather turned bad—indoors to play
I tried to make games and be a bold friend
Though strong was the call of the harsh winter wind

They ran out of doors and shouted and sang
(*They won't find us from the road*)
Their voices went soft as they ran further on
(*Thicker branches tangled so*)
Till only a trace of their singing did hang
(*Flashlights fading, the fire low*)
On my eyes and my whiskers where they didn't belong

Then my someone from childhood came into the room
And lay her wet head on my withering feet
Her tears wet my lap and she fell asleep soon
Saying nothing to me just going to sleep

O how my head burned as I sat unprepared
(*Come marry me here and then we'll go*)
I was rendered blind and of the world unaware
(*To the places in the snow*)
In the quiet of the day, well, I laid her low
(*You a fire, me aglow*)
And used her skin as my skin to go out in the snow

Italicized lyrics by Dawn McCarthy.

THERE IS NO GOD

There is no god

Except:
that which surrounds the tongue,
that which sees love in the chest,
that which puts mouth on cock and vagina . . .
well *that* that is best.

There is no prayer

Except:
That which is sung in laughter,
That which is lovingly uttered,
Or, through gritted teeth,
That which is hissed or muttered.

There is no god

But: There are those who will outlive you,
There is a force that is many,
There are teachings and taught,
There is tons!
There is one!
There is not any!

This song is written in English
and can't be translated
into dog.

272

THERE IS NO ONE WHAT WILL TAKE CARE OF YOU

Beneath a flow of water
You'll find yourself angling
You'll find the homewalk wetly

To spoil, you'll leave the day's catch,
While you drift off to sleep. . . .

"Hey, my baby
Don't drift away
Not on a sorry skull, o pal of mine
Don't let eyebrows settle permanently
Unfrowed with affection
Unafflicted by drama, what new can I say?
For the magic of my appearance does not exist you know

For the sake of somebody
You must rise and rhyme the rhyme we so despise
And do the task, the banal cleaning
Cast not a thought to your day of weaning
A vision hovers wild still o'er your head
mother sky is one of many for your heart
And the walls, the very walls that hinder vision
Act as windows on the skill
To fish
which is your art"

This is the end of the innocence.

THERE IS SOMETHING
I HAVE TO SAY

There is something I have to say
Because I'm leaving sometime today
And I can't tell when I'll be back

It's easy to imagine me here
The phone keeps a voice so near
But that kind of exchange hides the fact
That I'm going so very far
And today I know who you are
But tomorrow the space will make us other souls

Can we find communion again
In the bedroom or just as friends?
Is there difference between in lives like ours?

I feel deserving of love.
Can it be something I dispose of
Or put away in a box under the bed?
Will it rot there and spoil my days
Or recharge them in other ways?
Will it lift me to heights when I am dead?

What if I cannot live for you,
But for others still as I do?
How, then, will you absorb this word: goodbye?

There are no more leaving songs after this.

THERE WILL BE SPRING

There will be spring to the very end
I'll sleep to the sound of burning winter
I built a place for me and my friends
And they all walk by instead of enter
My father's house is gone and all
The houses in his town have crumbled
I am a child, ten inches tall,
And I have grown while they have stumbled
It pleases me to have your eyes
Close calmly moments after mine
And uncontrolled, your crazy thighs
Hold tighter to mine intertwined
For what will be ours to do today
Is to name everything that we see
After what we are and who came before
And the things that run in fear from you and me

Watch out, "There Will Be Winter" is
going to fuck you up.

THEY SAY SING WHAT YOU KNOW

They say sing what you know
And instead I've sung what I want
Some get right behind their history
And baby sometimes I just don't

When I look through that door   I say this ain't why
To the pain that came before   I've gone so high

    There are kings in my past
    And things no-one can be proud of
    I celebrate light that's cast
    And turn my face from any trace that shows lack of love

O when I look through that door   Here I go
I see me, nothing more   I'll sing what I know:

    I know better.

I know better than to be so proud
To take more love than I'm allowed
And hide it, cut if off from where it came
There's a force that brought me to this place
Power in the color of my face
I humbly say that Legend's just a name

I will sing what I know
I'm a man who stands on shoulders
Of my friends and all my heroes
Who insinuate a challenge to be bolder

I'll rise from the floor
And bust open that door
And if music chooses me to sing,
I'll let her
    I'll sing what I know:

I know better

written for John Legend to sing

THIS IS MY COCKTAIL

This is my cocktail
And I drink it 'cause
I love it
This is how I don't feel
And make friend of trouble

I fear two things:
Losing my mind
Losing my body

When you find your skin
Has been broke in
By thousand worms who
Cannot wait for you to be gone
Then you count to ten
And she looks upon your skin
And so begin to compose a vow:

Never hold a gun, nor a sign
It isn't fun, and fun is how you should define
One's way to be
Bedding down with twins
And hoping god will walk right in
And take a picture of
This holy group of three

It is enough to cry
It pays for all before you die
And kills the yearn to justify

I need two things:
Keeping my mind
Keeping my body

Merle sang: why can't I cry.
I wish they'd
given me crying lessons instead of, say, civics.

THREE PHOTOGRAPHS

There are only three photographs
Of me on the west coast
Entrusted to those hosts
Who held me out there

One shows me standing
By a brief sapling
One knee bending
Sullenly smoking

One is me holding
A length of chain
While on one cheek must
Be a streak of rust

In one other picture
One may only conjecture
How my constant protector
Could let me be so

Photographs do not represent
their subjects very well.

THREE QUESTIONS

1.

Say I found a piece of rock
And put it in my pocket
And for the day that we are wed
I put it in a locket
Which is to hang around your neck
As long as you see fit
Well, tell me, o my love
Do you think that you would wear it?

2.

And on a day that threatens
That the earth might open up
The birds have stopped their singing
And the insects have shut up
And all that's left between us
Is some al-hum-dil-lilly-lie
Would you split it with me, baby
So that I wouldn't die?

And after all these things
Is a question I must ask:

3.

When everyone has called me out
And said I am the worst
And asked for voices on my side
My love, would you sing first?
Would you say, "He's okay,

He's better than the rest;
He's innocent in god's eyes
And in mine, he is the best"?

This is a good song to sing when you are dejected.

TIME TO BE CLEAR

time to be clear
they told me he's gone and now I sing in your ear:
"no time to peel the wallpaper
& swing from chandelier
do something to show
that you know
it's time to be clear"

I can handle what's given
I can make mystry mine
and sing it with feeling
with rhythm & rhyme
and make you all marvel
that this is your time
and holler "it's time to be clear"

stop all the moaning &
bemoaning of fate
god isn't listening
or else it's too late
this is your song & your
song it is great
we're singing "it's time to be clear"

time to be clear
and leave our old worlds
& build new stories here
lover o lover o don't disappear
I will take care of you dear

Should be amply understandable, this song-within-a-song,
even as we are, from all sides,
encouraged to self-obfuscate.

TODAY I WAS AN EVIL ONE

Tonight my eyes were hurting much
As I had strained them all day long
I don't remember waking up
My memory is not that strong
The day was spent walking about
And asking questions blindly
And silently and not without
A sense of lapsing dignity

I was found again in need
And mostly unprotected
As I had spent good time with greed
And giving was rejected

The skin of all my fingers split
Painfully receding
My hands were dry and itched and hurt
And also they were bleeding
I can fix it by withdrawing
Claim from false completeness
And by humboly allowing
God to grant me sweetness

Today I was an evil one
Who suffered dumbly having fun
Tomorrow god will make me good
If I allow her to, she would

"Humboly" has an extra syllable, so that the
word does not slip by un-noticed.

TONIGHT'S DECISION
(AND HEREAFTER)

When's a crime forgiven by them?
You can never live it down
I can only advise to another
Never, o never forsake your brother

And where are my friends?
And where is my family?
They've all gone away
Though it's I who have left them

I have heard death cry, I have heard him falter
I have heard him lie and escape unscathed
When he comes for me I will fuck him, o
I will waste him in my own way
He is scum, but he wields great glory, o
O to live forever in some oceany glow
Let new life rise in the face of death
Let it rise, let it take in what can't be held
And with life, let me rise, let me stand up high
Let me then decide who all will die
For with me, I'd have all of everyone burn
And the rest suffer death in its own black blur

Let the others cry, while our voice is still
We will wait, we may lie like wolves in the fields
O hold your throats in silence a while
There is enough noise now from where they are
In the silence lie, in the silence take
O take in the rumor of a passing through
The house will be empty, a house of love
Calling out, there was nothing else for us to do

Where are the days
I used to be friendly?

This is comic-book dark.

TREASURE MAP

Treasure o treasure
A quiet mind
Don't even listen
Simply wait and you will find
A world in mourning
For an old world left behind
Parading, celebrating
Now respond in kind

My lord intones: you're made of bones

I get my strength from all the love that comes my way
And if we're brave, it's that we have the chance to say:
"I own this moment & keep loneliness at bay
By giving all of what I can during my stay"

My demon screams: I'm made of dreams

Sell your mind
And buy new eyes
Sell old ideas & buy surprise
Trade wisdom in
And look again, at treasure

Treasure,
A loser's pay
Love til it hurts or it will all go away
Pleasure o pleasure is the order of the day
Then ordered up against a wall and fire away

Fire away
Fire away
All away
Huzzah hooray!

Written for a motion picture called *The Lure.*

TROUBLESOME HOUSES

I once loved a girl, but she couldn't take that I visited
    troublesome houses.
She'd say, when I got home, to leave her alone.

She could taste trouble on my mouth.

When she was gone I missed her, I did . . . and still went to
    troublesome places.
I couldn't withstand a glorious day without seeing these trou-
    blesome faces.

And quiet eluded me, and keeps from me still, though I need
    my own bed and its solace.
Day's noises steal in and copper my will, and I face the evils
    that follow us.

I once had a house, and my family knew where to find me if
    ever they needed.
Troublesome houses were foreign to them.
They thought all Papa's orders I heeded.
Now they can't find me; they don't have my numbers, and just
    hear reports of my doings.

Troublesome houses are not in their minds, though it's in those
    I do all my moving.

                     Show me a house not full of trouble.

TRUDY DIES

I haven't been sad now
For so many years
With no foe to fight
Death's all I feared
'Cause death could take you
Death could take you
And that's just what it do
That's just what it do

A bird in my ear
Was beaking away
About all the jewels
He'd come across that day
Jewels in the grass
Where the worms used to be

The cattle were lowing
They cried for your feet
The clouds were your arches
The cows were asleep
And they spoke of you
They spoke of you
As they laid there and mooed
As they lay there and "moo"

The house walls are tighter
The bed it is small
Housing just one soul
Just one soul at all
Where it once held two
It once held two
Now it doesn't hold you
Now it doesn't hold you

The ride and I won't be
Towards working today
That's good, that's over
You are away
And now I'll undo
Now I'll undo
That's just what I'll do
That's just what I'll do

Dreams put us through
the paces, prepare us
for what could or should
happen and songs can do
that, too.

TURKEY VULTURE

I'm a turkey vulture
On a big Appaloosa
In a ship going downhill with all sails blown
And I'll soar and I'll sail
I will flap for to fly
'Cause life is a ball, then you die.

The time is nigh for bold strokes
By bold folks and deputies

When I got to Wyoming
There was a woman there waiting
With scissors in her hand and a devious grin
She sat me down in a chair
And she then cut my hair
And now I'm a good-looking guy.

Throw consideration out the door
And pull your nearest loved one to the floor.
And then pull on your pants
Straighten my tie
I'm the best lay that money can buy.

My first song.

TWO MORE DAYS

Just two more days
'Til we should have said "I do."
And you'd slip out of your shoes at Niagara.

Oh those falls would have amazed us
Sleepless nights of love sure would have dazed us
High prices and poor service wouldn't have fazed us
We'd slap 'em twenty percent any old way.

Two more days
Just two more days
'Til our families would gather
And you'd have said I'd rather
not meet your aunt.

You said I wouldn't have liked her if I met her
When two days now is up I will forget her
If she tries to change your mind, don't you let her
'Cause I've sold your ticket and bought me a barrel

Two more days
'Til I'll ride these awesome falls
Wearing wooden overalls
at Niagara.

A JACKASS SPURNED

UNDER WHAT WAS OPPRESSION

You do not have to be ignorant
For me to get on with you
Rather you do
If anything is to shine through

Brainless to me is broad and bold in most ways
Playful when scowling
Your manner betrays you

Before you wake up
I am making my living
Breathing and cursing
Misbehaving

God has given me no gift
To speak honestly to myself
Or to decide strongly in another's company

Tonight I think of her
When where she is was said to be a possible place
Some friends of mine would head to

I cannot decide
Work will do it for me
And I will not know yet
If she chooses to ignore me

We haven't gotten smarter
over the years. We never
never will become smarter!

UNTITLED

"did you like the cake?"
"aw, some of it was nice
I have made a cake like that
in my own home once or twice
just as fine as that one
which we had some of today
none of it was wonderful
much morely okay"

"then you can make another
if you know what is wrong
but I am too distracted
from fighting all day long
but I will help you do it
I will come and meet you here
but where may I then find you on
this corner of the stair?"

into her head a figure:
six o'clock exact
and if she did not come down
it would have been no fact
the truth is of the moment
the believer is to blame
if some off-handed statement
brings thoughtfulness and shame

Roofing nails like popcorn poppers.

VALENTINE'S DAY

It's Valentine's Day, and I'm catatonic
And only over the sea will that be taken

And oh, I could be (the possibilities)
And oh, I could be (the possibilities)
And oh, I could be (the possibilities)

God has made you one face,
you must find another
God has made you one face,
you must find
you must be born again

> This song is 100 percent from others, for others,
> and so I *love* it.

VIVA ULTRA

She's my lifeblood, she's my secret sharer,
always been around this place.
And when I call her,
It's not long before she comes to where I'm calling from.
Do I hate her?
Do I know her just to hate what she does?

Are you jealous of the show we put on?
Are you wary?
Is there justice?
Is there something which resembles pleasure?
And are you mammals?
Do you eat and drink the same as we do?

Oh! it's okay not to say.

Is there time still? Time to forage for a decent dinner here?
Where we've settled . . .
where we've come to call the new century in?

And when I wake up
I do not ask her
If she knows just where we lay ourselves.
It's better that way. And so it's this way
that we start our day today.

Russ Meyer & Andrei Tarkovsky

WAI

The lameness of an unborn child
The tidiness of cry
The only way I'm leaving here is curling up and die

The way our shelter moves above
Controlled by just my hand
Insures the death you're dreaming of
The drowning down of man

O love, o love, o careless love
I only want to lay with you
My love, my love, my careful love
I've found the hard way love is true

Always love the smiling one
And rounding out will come
With bitter bile and heartless fun
And consciousness made numb

And fearful hate that's stemming out
From fear and only fear
Has made your inner croco shout
And bring his victims here

O love, o love, o careless love
I only want to lay with you
My love, my love, my careful love
I've found the hard way love is true

A creature born in listlessness
His hatred to become
It's here his love is swollen in
And consciousness made numb

And relegate your youth and trust
Your table and your skin
And share the love the godly must
And hold it 'til the end

O love, o love, o careless love
I only want to lay with you
My love, my love, my careful love
I've found the hard way love is true

Down with extroversion!

WATER

For a swim, I'd wager, for a swim
I'd trade my own mother in
If you'd point me a lake
Less a moment it would take
For to find me treading within

For the sea, I'd bargain, for the sea
If there was a thing missed by me
It's the much-honored chance
Just to have this last dance
With a column of watery spray

For a drink
Please someone just a drink
Just one swallow before I sink
In the cradling limbs of the demon what swims
'neath the oceanic tumble of think

Trying to find these words, I came
upon a recording from 1993 of a
show in a small city in Belgium. The
second line of the third stanza was
an honest-to-goodness plea to the
audience, à la Bodeco, and the resulting
lyric is a significant improvement
on the original.

THE WAY

Winter comes and snow
I can't marry you, you know
Without children to grow
I can't marry you, you know

Love me the way i love you

Take a year in your hands
You can find another man
Let your unloved parts get loved
I will be your man

Love me the way i love you

Places you should be afraid
Into the river we will wade

Love me the way i love you

The way to get to the top
is to get off of your bottom.

WE ALL, US THREE, WILL RIDE

In a small, far room the bed is set
With trinkets all surrounding
Yet lone it rests, so dry it sets
With souls aside abiding
There moves legs warm and close inside
Though no leg braces a hello
And pictures on walls where paint is lain
Where sinks are friendly running

Reflect, reflect metal cast
My toe has long been swollen
My knees are blue, my eyes are too
My love has not forgotten
Will come, will come, o he will come
And make me have a baby
Then I foresee we all, us three,
will ride and all together

The hills have eyes, the trees have lives
Disjointed like a hero
No saga told, no things unfold
To make the ride much finer
The length is fine, his hand in mine
Does someone hear our chatter?
A lover's laugh, a bleating calf
A dog out in the harbor

                              No great shakes,
                    just one eventless incarnation.

WE ARE UNHAPPY

we are unfound
we are unseen
nothing is coming
nothing is clean

earth it is shaking
people have fled
& lord she is taking
the eyes from the dead
demonized body
exorcised mind
pieces of kindness
exchanged in kind

mind it is going, faith is destroyed
emptiness showing god's cruelty deployed
lovers have left, friends close their eyes
children bereft
we all are unwise

nothing is better
nothing is best
we are unhappy
we are unblessed

we are unhappy

Dementia can really
tear people apart.

WEAKER SOLDIER

I once was a weaker soldier hanging in the war
But I left, like an ape folded neatly in four
And silently prayed for a moment slow and bled
On a sandalwood bust I had
Where was the field where I had pressed another down?
Where I had revealed myself by crying and shouting?
I turned away from that and into this black kettle of one-ness

I have not been feeling the same
I am not fit to carry your name
I am not fit and I am not willing
To go on

Sold down the lane, in a way to restrain
You from calling a name and then regretting.
If you save what you own you are always alone
And then why postpone the good death?
We are those who break laws when the cold body thaws
Who prefer breaking jaws but must lower ourselves.
Unfit though we are to help you get very far,
Still we would never mar your rightful due.

I have not been feeling the same
I am not fit to carry your name
I am not fit and I am not willing
To go on

It was noon before she moved into the yard and pressed her
      hair
With a hand yellowed, smooth, and shaking.
She had pulled on a housedress over nothing but her skin
And stood in the grass looking about her.
You breathe in here, and you've breathed of me.

My girl here, she loves you, she'll take you upstairs.
Call on me later, much later in life,
But do me a favor and leave her up there.

I am not feeling the same.
I am not willing to carry your name.
I am not here, and I am not going
To be there.

If workers in song are
soldiers, then we
are also drill sergeants,
and cowardly generals
with maps on walls
far away from enemy lines.

WE LOVE OUR HOLE

It's ours for causing trouble
And ours for painting town
Amidst the blister's bubble
My baby's back is brown
My baby's ball is bouncing
To a cove where love is free
Sunshine song is pouncing
Having me sing out with glee:
We love our hole!

Crazy to be living
Where a rain dance can be sung
No bullshit I am giving
It's so hard to speak without a tongue

And we're *in* it, but not *of* it
We are human and above
We have scored the means to love it
And spent the spoils on yet more love
We love our hole!

Simply is as simply we do

You'll never understand:
We're good to explore our hole

Not to cry when something ends
Not to boast when luck's inflating
Not to tell on foes or friends
For to tell is devastating

We love our hole!

I admire and marvel at the strenuous
localism that allows someone to tattoo
her postal code onto her neck.
If she would just arm herself
to keep our influence out, something
might be preserved.

WERNER'S LAST BLUES
TO BLOKBUSTER

In the old town
When I last came around
Things were not so obvious
She was not parading as she had

Werner, he whispered to me:
"Marriage is bliss.
It's something that I've skirted around
But that I don't plan to miss."

But stuck in a corner
She was seen stumbling over there
"I washed my hands of him,
But he thought I was washing my hair!"
Unrecognizably red,
I slipped through the scene.
Out on the street there was no time
To pause or look back.

It's better to be
So far off from thee,
Where I recall you pleasantly;
Where I can feel free.
Now I wander aimlessly,
No light on in the hall,
No friendly step a-steering me,
No guiding hand at all.

O Blokbuster
O Blok
Waiting to know
Waiting to see
Waiting to go,
I was waiting for thee.

I had a story about these brothers,
this one is from the middle brother
who has gone as far as he can
with what he was given.
He expects the world to take over
where his folks left off, but the world
doesn't love him like that, not at all.

WEST PALM BEACH

I can't get the sand out of my shoes.
This being in Florida's done a number on my blues.
Just the way the women walk 'round here . . .
It's plain to see the way the sand and sea have done a number
    on me.
And the sky is threatening black and gray
And the sun's a festering red
And her head is claiming her stats, she ain't yet risen from bed.
So breakfast again: delayed, postponed.
I won't be fed.

The surf has swallowed him up,
He's a memory now.
And the water is warmer than it has been in weeks.
And Grandma lives just down the road,
She's making supper for me tonight.
She's been nice to me since '73
When her son lost his lights.
And now his ghost is a rising host above the briny blur.
I would that soon
Some maid would swoon
And his soul would capture her.
He's still a fine kid, what with all that he did.
(He's a fan of mine.)

I wasn't planning to spend so long in town,
But the break in the weather has got the partner down.
She won't get out,
She's shotgun,
Seems she's sewn to the seat.
It's a dirty trick that I've yet to lick
And that she has yet to beat.

And you can see in her eyes, she was born unwise,
She was born for me.
If she mourns too long, I'll know something's wrong
And I'll leave her be.

You could tell by his shoes, he was born to lose.
He was also born for me.

Following a strict
recipe for escapism.

WESTERN SONG

Where will you go
Now that you know?
Where will you go
Now that you know?

Never once did you say
That you cared
If I went anywhere

Friendly ghosts are still dead
and unable to find peace.
This is what they sing
when we aren't watching.

WHAT ARE YOU?

What are you waiting for / if not for me?
What are you waiting for? it must be me.

To take you over my knee
And spank you mercilessly
I can do that / oh you'll see

And every day will be like three
And sleep: adventure
you will see
And I'll have you and you'll have me

On a bench / with your twisted fingers in me
In the rain / with my sundress torn off of me
Sliding down grassy slopes / where we can be alone

You say I am evil / You know that I'm stupid
I don't appear giving / And I don't appear lucid
Yet I give you all
The truth is / I give you everything

When we don't receive enough
punishment as children,
we inflict more than our
share as adults.

313

WHAT'S MISSING IS

What's missing is
What's missing is
What's missing is

Some kind of pillow
Some loving willow
Some care once denied
Now dissolved inside

What's plenty is
What's plenty is
What's plenty is

One god
Six tongues
Five breaths
Four lungs

What's rhythm is
What's rhythm is
What's rhythm is

Plenty of things missing
Steps taken, lips kissing
New harmony on an awesome scale
Meat against meat, under sail

What's missing remains
missing until the
missing itself is gone.

WHAT'S WRONG WITH A ZOO?

what's wrong with a zoo?

I asked them in. Invited them in,
oh cordially.

Sat each one down,
down on the couch,
so I could see

what's wrong with a zoo.

Show me some skin
kiss on my chin
and kiss my mouth.
I learned the way
to love you today
was to have you down.

Monkey was maimed;
black and white aim . . .
a chimp no more.
Monkey's last act
had been to attack
a child of four.

what's wrong with a zoo?

So I pile misdeed upon misdeed,
throw in some love
where I see need of love.
An eloquent way to bring an end
is exit the bay
in graceful swim.

A box folds in half
and brings on a laugh
from everyone.
Who needs to sleep
when sleeping just keeps
our lives undone?

what's wrong with a zoo?

One of the more disturbing
paradoxes of human civilization
is when a zoo-kept animal
is shot for attacking
a human being.

WHERE IS THE PUZZLE

Where is the puzzle that bothers me so?
How do I let my family know?
O I'm disappearing into the wind
I knew everything once and now I know it all again:
Bliss comes with conclusion
Comes with an end

Hear our voices
Pass it on
Knowledge is born with a singing dawn

Goodbye and welcome, troubled song
My body fades . . . your life goes on
And I want only you
And I trust only you
And I want only to
Sing you

a self-guided tour through
the mysteries of Don Everly
yields more mysteries

WHERE WIND BLOWS

From here where wind blows
I'm waiting to know
What I'll never know:
What you think of me.

You send me pictures and words of love
I am an older boy
There's nothing I'm sure of
'Cept I know
I have faith to soar
strength to fly
and little more.

Wind has worn from me: hostility,
Gentility . . . I wear like a crown.

Imagine me otherwise!
A hundred guys would kill to be walking beside you here

So it isn't clear what's wrong with me.

I get my feet wet.
I pay my debt.
I am loved.
Yet. . . .
What do you think of me?

You bring me melodies and hand over gold rings
With silver keys,
Say I'm your lover.
O why do you think of me?

For boys who play with jacks
or jump rope or make
spider webs out of yarn.

WHIPPED

Yes I'm quieter, tireder
More apt to say
"You go on, boys. I'm good,
think I'll stay in today."
I ain't older . . .
Yes I'm older.
But that's not why the scales have tipped

O you know I've been chosen
To be whipped

Lion-tamer
Pride / life re-framer
That warm pot of gold
Always waiting
Fear-abating
To welcome me home from the cold

It's my pleasure
O my treasure
It's the opening that I
Had so dreamed for
Often screamed for
I was as like to die
Then I found her
Now I hound her
To get mine fully-lipped
I'm in love, love
And I'm absolutely
Whipped

Must be love!
I'm whipped and cowed
I'll whoop and holler
(If I'm allowed)

Clinging to the future,
every aspect of it.

WHITHER THOU GOEST

A sickroom hush, a holiday glow
Whither thou goest I will go
Whither thou wish inside,
We will follow

It is to be on one thing only
On the road to God knows where
Some are happy, some are laden
And those wish death upon themselves

Here is law, it is spoken
In a growl choked
Her paws have strayed in her sleep
And in my mouth are cloaked
The claws-fists which deny themselves a shallowness
And which recall the television or the room alone
In which they preened unmoving towards
My loving tongue

Convolutions may arise
The skull is echoing with webs
And the third wave flushed the thing out
Everybody jump and shout!

Scream my name above the din,
Above the engine's carnal din
Above the calves who bleat their lungs out:
"Baa baa,
moo moo,
baa baa baa."

If you sleep with dogs,
you wake, eventually,
with puppies.

A WHOREHOUSE IS ANY HOUSE

there's a woman I see at a bar that's near me
who catches my eye repeatedly
and so it's one evening, I wait until four
when the bar turns its lights out and closes the door

and then I may follow her cautiously home
where she would go walking or stumbling alone
and I can't help but want to see her at her window
and to want to approach her and stand just below

and I needed so much to have nothing to touch
and I wanted so dear to have nothing so near
and to render the city unbounded and pretty
so to slip in and out of her and then to slip off

goodbye to the city, goodbye to the girl
her room is left standing, her room is my world
and in it she slips into bed without thinking
and I follow closely for I have been drinking

and slip in beside her and she doesn't stir so
I settle up closer and warmer to her
and so the night passes and so the sun comes
as we sleep and we wonder on what we have done

> A Peeping Tom's child
> rebels: "My dad
> was a wimp!"

WILLOW TREES BEND

Willow trees bend
but I won't bend
I will never lay down
for every man alive
there's a fire
and for every king a crown

my world's been rocked before
and it will be rocked again
by a tremor or a howling wind
and lord if you demand
if the world at large asks of me
I will surrender to you

fun and joy the aim
so we live forever
they may mock us, but we do
the river carries on
clouded with what we've done
the deeds of me and you

we have a power
all animals do
when faced with your fire
I will surrender to you

One of the first unexpected purely musical
invitations took me to Brittany
where I heard Mary Margaret
O'Hara for the first time. This
triangulates her words with
black metal and advertisement.

324

WITH CORNSTALKS OR AMONG THEM

Where were you again tonight?
(with cornstalks or among them)
Moonless night my love burned bright
(o out among them).

I'm not impressed by fields of cane.
Our house is good to me, and plain.
Happiness can live here still,
if coming back you only will.

Or I can find you out among
(o out among them)
and sleep next to you
and hear it sung
(o out among them).

I have saved enough that I can go.
But where to find you,
I don't know.
Please to find me,
here I am,
devoured by fields
unmade by man.

You love me still,
although it's strange.
Will you love me if I change?

There was one life with you before . . .
and one life more,
one life more.

　　　　　　　　　　　it was with sugarcane, but
　　　　　　　　　　　then the corn grew so high

WOLF AMONG WOLVES

She loves a soul that I have never been
A dog among dogs,
A man among men,
And every day
When I come home to her
She holds a phantom,
She kisses and she hugs him,
And I am not averse to how she loves him.
But why must I live and walk
Unloved as what I am?

Why can't I be loved as what I am?
A wolf among wolves
And not as a man among men?

She craves a hole that she can go in,
A sheltered cave that I have never seen,
Not in my life,
Not even in my dreams.

Built to be a massive
country hit.

WORK HARD, PLAY HARD

Don't you know that I work hard?
Don't you know that I play hard?
Don't you know it's a hard way?
Trace the bus lines in the state . . .
Don't you know that I see she'd strip for me?

Well we're moving around.
Me 'n' she have a grasp on coming down.
And we do it the same,
In the name of glory, filth, and fame.
Things are going okay.
We find a little puppy love makes the day;
Once in the morning . . . and once at night.

Me and Frankie we cry some evenings outside where we lie:
Will another one come? Will we go tonight into the sun?
So to couple anew . . .
Times like that, it's the only thing to do.

Once in the morning
and once at night.

Most folks think that writers,
singers, artists don't really
work. "Most folks" includes
most writers, singers, artists.

YOU ARE LOST

It was bound to happen
From when you first knew you
And pulled apart, with will,
From those around you.

If you love wind,
Or morning or night,
If you are kind,
And get lit up by light
Then you're bound to be put down at any cost.
And if you listen to me
You are lost.

You are lost as I am singing.
You are lost inside a sound.
If you can get away from these words ringing
Maybe you can be found.

If your heart tells you that you love
And you listen,
And you know a purpose holds you in your place,
I only ask you: close your eyes that you won't see me.
Then light will shine fully on your face.

Buyer beware: don't look behind
the curtain.

YOU ARE SEEN

You have been seen in what you do;
In fact, I'm the one who has seen you.

I've seen you be you;
What a shame that someone had to.

I've seen your eyes wide
When you've felt others' power
Start to slide.

I've seen your eyes wide
When you've found your real access
To Love subside.

I've seen your pulse rise
As you've seen
The deadening of eyes.

You have been seen in what you do;
In fact I'm the one who has seen you.

I've seen your step lighten,
Your throat tighten,
In unashamed revival.
Your blood race,
Your slack face,
In unashamed denial.

You have been seen in what you do;
In fact, I'm the one who has seen you.

Increased surveillance will not
diminish dark habits.

YOU CAN LIKE IT

sing to me anyone
sing hard, sing out
harmonize happiness
with fear and doubt
and use the whole song
to cleave the rock
pull hands from pockets
and the key from the lock

placing stone upon stone to have
a fortress where it's finally safe to laugh
you build a masterpiece and all the while
lose any claim to see your children smile

oh you can like it
but you can't come in
there is no there there
its love is just pretend
it seemed astounding
and didn't feel so far
oh turn around babe
the love was where you are

Most solutions sought through
song will call for excruciating
translation before they can
be of any real use.

YOU CAN REGRET WHAT
YOU HAVE DONE

You can regret what you have done
What you have not can be more fun
But what you've done can't be undone
It can be buried by new deeds
But will soak through each time you bleed
And so betray what you have done
You can't claim to be a holy sun
You are a freak, you are a beast
What was the peak became the least
And, crippled, you must own your place
Your unexceptional owned space
You can regret what you have done
Those unchallenged are lucky ones
For what we do when we are tried
Is likely let our good selves die
And then from bottom we rebuild
Use every bone that was not killed
To make an unbeatable one
Already mauled and crushed, and gone
And now the excess chipped away
The new creation left to say
Some kids may fear not having fun
But you'll regret what you have done
O you'll regret what you have done

Imagine
some young person who
believes that s/he can
measure accomplishment.

332

YOU CAN'T HURT ME NOW

I know everyone knows the trouble I have seen;
That's the thing about trouble you can love.
Everyone has the eyes and ears to be where I have been.
You can have that heaven here
And not wait for up above.

The more I feel myself,
The more alone I am.
Though you can't hurt me now
I still fear God's plan.

I know everyone has the happiness I have;
That's the thing about happiness that you can hold.
Everyone has had the sense of my own belly laugh;
That's the heaven here at hand that does not grow old.

The more I feel myself,
The more you're close to me.
Though you can't hurt me now
I still fear destiny.

It don't have to be known someday;
Let's know it now and not let someday get in the way.

By zip-lining from here to
wherever it is Madonna may be,
not only are unparalleled
views witnessed but also
a thrilling ride can be had.

YOU DON'T LOVE ME

I wanted a woman who loves who I am and what I do.
Then I met you.
You couldn't care less if I was lord of Japan,
Or half a man
Nor what I am.

You say you like my eyes only
Or just the way I giggle.
Sometimes you like the smell of me
Or how my stomach jiggles.
But you don't love me.
That's alright, because you cling to me all through the night.

I wanted to grow old with one who knew me inside-out
And likes to shout things I'm about.
But you just turn your head when I get rowdy like a child,
And you don't even crack a smile.

You say my kissing rates a six on a scale of one to ten,
And you wouldn't pass the time with me
Except you're tired of all your friends.
And you don't love me.
That's alright,
Because you cling to me
All through the night.

Gut-bucket, department-store good times.

YOU HAVE CUM IN YOUR HAIR
AND YOUR DICK IS
HANGING OUT

A head start on the frog
On the deer and the dog
The things we true were taught
Loyal torn from our heart

It's now so soft underfoot
We sleep more than we sleep
If god could make me cry
I'd run along the water

She won't come
I'll be gone
She won't come
I'll be gone

Play with it while you have hands
A desperate lack of demands
I can't offer a thing
Better than dying, so take it

Scrap the outfit
And hand me the keys to your car
If I leave before it is light
I'll be around when you are

She won't come
I'll be gone
She won't come
I'll be gone

A song without a title meets
a title without a song. Built with Bryan Rich. He made the
chorus and the second verse.

YOU WANT ME TO (CONQUER)

They'd left me behind.
I thought I was on my own.
When I looked around,
I found I was not alone.
Everybody had a way
Of saying I was wrong.
I'd step into a circle and
They'd all say I don't belong.

In the low wet night
I changed into
A hero of those starved of light,
Starved of power to pull on through.

I'm a conquer now!
And I always was.
What's different now
Is I conquer because

You want me to
You want me to
You want me to

> In the voice of John the Conquer,
> an elusive figure. Trying to
> nail him to a tree, to
> tickle him.

337

YOU WANT THAT PICTURE

What did you do when you saw that I'd gone?
Did you stand very still
and
did tears come falling?

O you want that picture, don't you darling?
of poor little me standing there bawling.
Well, it's true that I cried,
but then I went outside
and I stood very still in the night
and I looked at the sky
and knew someday I'd die
and then everything would be all right.

IT'S ALL RIGHT.
AND EVERYTHING COMES DOWN TO THIS:
THAT EVERYTHING THERE EVER WAS
OR WILL BE
IS ALL THERE IS.

Where did you go once you'd wrote me that note
was a weight lifted off of your shoulders
did you fly?

O you want that picture, don't you darling?
of heartless cold me
flying not falling.
Well, it's true that I soared
but then I went outdoors
and I stood very still in the night

and I looked at the sky
and knew someday I'd die
and then everything would be all right

WHEN YOU DON'T EVEN KNOW WHO I AM EVEN
MORE THAN I.

YOU WILL MISS ME WHEN
I BURN

In the corners there is light
That is good for you
In behind you, I have warned you,
There are awful things
Will you miss me when I burn?
And will you close the others' eyes?
It would be such a favor
If you would blind them

Will you miss me when I burn?
And will you eye me with a longing?
It is longing that I feel
To be missed,
Or to be real
There is absence, there is lack,
There are wolves here abound.
You will miss me when I turn around.

An obsession with light, dark, and
emotional osmosis begins here. The chorus,
omitted above, was made by Bryan Rich and states:
"When you have no-one,
no-one can hurt you."

YOU WIN

I don't have any more fight left in me
Been punched to the left and hooked on what's free
And when I see that look of battle on tonight
I know that I don't have time to fight

Let the air be like rain and the moon go away
God delivers just pain and just pain has had its day
I will put my hands
where all eyes can see I've no threat to deliver
so leave old Bonny be

When deception returns and anger holds sway
Oh, push me aside and say you will not play.
I will go where you go and listen again
Oh darling, I'll lean in and sing softly
You win

One of the benefits of aging
is the prerogative
to stop fighting.

ACKNOWLEDGMENTS

I take this opportunity to acknowledge many collaborators who have equal right to authorship and ownership for a number of the whole songs of which the lyrics in this collection are a part, most significantly Emmett Kelly, Matt Sweeney, and Mick Turner, but also Blake Mills, Bryan Rich, Valgeir Sigurðsson, David Byrne, and Chris Vrenna.

There was a previous collection of lyrics, privately pressed, called *Royal Stable Words* Vol. 1; it was illustrated and hand-printed by Diane Radford, hand-bound by Eugene Ward, in an edition of three hundred.

For this book, gratitude is due to the folks at Norton, especially editor Tom Mayer. Also thanks go to literary agent Chris Parris-Lamb for the hauling of paving stones to make this road clear and scenic. Olivia Wyatt and Jefferson Holt greased the wheels at pivotal times.

Boundless credit and appreciation I owe to the assemblages of able and inspired folks at Drag City, Domino, Spunk, Billions, and CNL, as well as other companies and individuals involved with the building of the life of all of this music.

And thank you Elsa.